The Golden Age of Piracy

Williamsburg in America Series

VII

*The seventh in a series of popular histories
of Williamsburg and Tidewater Virginia in
the eighteenth century.*

HISTORIE DER ZEE-ROOVERS.

THE
GOLDEN AGE
OF PIRACY

BY

Hugh F. Rankin

COLONIAL WILLIAMSBURG

WILLIAMSBURG, VIRGINIA

Distributed by

HOLT, RINEHART AND WINSTON, INC.

NEW YORK

HOLT, RINEHART AND WINSTON SBN: 03–081018–3

COLONIAL WILLIAMSBURG SBN: 910412–00–6

Distributed simultaneously in Canada by
Holt, Rinehart and Winston of Canada, Limited

Printed in the United States of America

For my sister
ANNE

PREFACE

The Golden Age of Piracy is a study of piracy as practiced by English-men, primarily off the coast of the North American colonies, and the activities of pirates in such busy corners of the globe as Madagascar and the Red Sea therefore have been minimized.

Most of the major pirates of the so-called "Golden Age" found good hunting off the Virginia capes. In general, the most active period of freebooting was over by 1730, although occasional notices of pirates occurred well into the nineteenth century and, indeed, pirates still lurk today in certain remote waters of the world. Eventually, I suppose, there will be space pirates when men begin to travel celestial highways with greater frequency.

Because pirates were a restless lot, they switched captains and crews as their fancies dictated, making this a difficult story to put together in a chronological fashion. Some, after serving their apprenticeships with well-established captains and crews, gathered their own followers about them and sailed forth with their own "gang." This results in a seeming reincarnation, for pirates who are hanged in one chapter often make a reappearance in subsequent accounts. And one would guess that many of the more successful pirates seldom appeared in the contemporary records, for most of the extant information appears in the records of those who were captured, tried, and executed.

A number of people have offered valuable aid. Mrs. Georgia C. Haugh and William S. Ewing of the William L. Clements Library of the University of Michigan; Mr. William Powell of the North Carolina Collection of the Louis R. Wilson Library of the University of North Carolina; Mr. John L. Lochhead, Librarian, The Mariners Museum; and

Mrs. Rose Belk of the Library of Colonial Williamsburg, Inc., all were most helpful in searching out materials. Dr. George Reese of the Department of Research of Colonial Williamsburg gave the manuscript a careful reading and made a number of valuable suggestions that saved me from several grievous errors. I hope that the end result is worthy of their aid.

HUGH F. RANKIN

New Orleans

CONTENTS

ILLUSTRATIONS

The Golden Age of Piracy

I

PRINCES OF THE SEA

*"those that were poor and had nothing but from
hand to mouth turned pirates...."*

Long before 1607, when the English established their first permanent
settlement in the New World at Jamestown in Virginia, piracy
flourished off the North American coast. In truth, it might be stated that
the earlier settlements in America encouraged piracy. But piracy was not
a product of America. Ever since man began to use water for the
transportation of worldly wealth, his greed led him to seek ways to
plunder and rob travelers of the sea.

Early recorded history takes notice of pirates; the Bible notes those
"Princes of the sea" who struck terror into the hearts of honest travelers.
Julius Caesar held a first-hand knowledge of *pirata;* he was captured and
held for ransom by Mediterranean corsairs. It should be noted, however,
that Caesar, once ransomed, returned and overwhelmed his captors while
they were still boisterously celebrating their good fortune. He cut their
throats before he crucified them. Piracy was a partial cause for Caesar's
invasion of Britain; in order to completely put down the Veneti pirates of
Brittany, he had first to subdue the Britons who furnished many men to
the Veneti crews.

The Vikings, or "sea-warriors," were early pirates along the coasts of
western Europe. They were a systematic body of freebooters, operating
under a strictly enforced code of conduct. From 789 A.D. on, they carried
out annual raids along the coasts of England, Scotland, and Ireland,

intermarrying with the native women and establishing colonies. From these settlements, raids were conducted against the continent, and by 912 A.D. they had conquered Normandy. With continued success, these people gradually spread to Spain and thence into Mediterranean waters.

In the year 1241 the cities of Hamburg and Lübeck combined and, with other German cities later joining with them, formed the Hanseatic League, a combination that grew into one of the great trading organizations of the Middle Ages. To protect their trade from the pirates of England, the League employed mariners to aid in the suppression of the freebooters. These men only added to the general problem, however, for many of them, in turn, became pirates.

The Hanseatic League likewise encouraged piracy in a less subtle manner when it employed, or made alliances with, pirates in its wars against Waldemar IV, King of Denmark. So numerous did these corsairs become that eventually the league had to employ an entire fleet to damp the enthusiasm of the sea robbers.

During the late Middle Ages England's trade grew—and so did piracy in the English Channel. The weak, almost non-existent Royal Navy was so ineffectual that trading communities were forced to protect themselves rather than look to the Crown for help. The five port towns of Hastings, Romney, Hythe, Dover, and Sandwich, the first of the Cinque Ports, banded together to suppress piracy and to police the Channel. Later the towns of Winchelsea and Rye were added. For their efforts the Cinque Ports were granted a number of privileges, not the least of which was the right to plunder all non-English ships passing through the Channel. Under such sweeping rights, it was but a step to the plunder of all seafarers alike, regardless of nationality. Even some of the officials of the Cinque Ports engaged in pirating merchant vessels flying the English flag. With this example before them, the inhabitants of other port towns began to turn to piracy as a path to sudden wealth.

As the years went by, piracy in the English Channel fluctuated inversely with the strength of the British navy and the resolution of the reigning monarch. It managed to survive the years of Henry VIII's efforts to build up England's navy, and had assumed something of an air of respectability by the time Elizabeth I ascended the throne.

One factor influencing the increase in piracy was the brash international politics of the era. Wars, threats of wars, and constant attempts to weaken a potential enemy in times of peace gave rise to the practice of privateering. In essence, privateering was little more than legalized piracy. Privateers were privately owned ships, officered and manned by civilians and commissioned as naval vessels by the government through a letter of marque. Used against the shipping of a hostile or potentially hostile nation, privateers were, in fact, auxiliaries of the Royal Navy. Inasmuch as the chief personal objective of privateering was the quick accumulation of wealth, these vessels were employed primarily against merchant shipping. A portion of the plunder went to the Crown. Then, after the deduction of all operating costs, the owners, officers, and men shared in the spoils.

Privateering in England began as early as the thirteenth century. Edward I (1272–1307) granted "Commissions of Reprisal" to owners of merchant ships that had been plundered illegally at sea. To recoup their losses, the holders of the commissions were entitled to plunder any merchantman they could take flying the same flag as their predators. It should be noted that these commissions were issued in times of peace as well as in periods of war, and as an accepted method of reprisal they dated back to the ancient Greeks. Later, privateers became private men-of-war, outfitted and armed by adventurous men of fortune.

By the middle of the sixteenth century Queen Mary (1552–1558), was more interested in restoring Catholicism to her realm and holding the affection of her husband, Philip II of Spain, than she was in the international welfare of England. She allowed the navy to deteriorate to such a weak state that piracy thrived in the Channel without benefit of commissions.

England's policy toward both Rome and Spain was reversed when Elizabeth I came to the throne. Pirates became tools of national policy and received some covert official support. Freebootery had become a business, and many of its operations were controlled through rather complex syndicates, which planned voyages and arranged for necessary bribes. It has been estimated that by 1562 some 400 pirate ships swarmed the English Channel.

These pirates became, in a sense, a privileged criminal class. Even though the Spanish Ambassador spent much of his time at the English court protesting the activities of these people against his country's shipping, those prominent Englishmen called before the Privy Council were always exonerated of any wrongdoing. Although most of their activities were directed against Spanish vessels sailing to the Netherlands, they were not above plundering English fishing and coastal vessels that fell into their hands. Even then, those who were apprehended seldom suffered the penalties of the law. Some mysteriously escaped from jail; others were acquitted by the courts. This permissive attitude stemmed from the fact that Elizabeth was attempting to rebuild her navy to defend England from an almost certain attack by Spain. Not only did the pirates provide a degree of defense for England, but they furnished a manpower pool of experienced, battle-tested seamen to man the men-of-war once they were launched.

The most famous pirate of the day (although no man is a pirate unless he is so termed by his contemporaries) was Sir Francis Drake, usually styled as one of the Elizabethan "Sea Dogs," who were themselves little more than pirates. Drake systematically plundered the towns and galleons of Spain's New World empire. His round-the-world voyage evolved from a scheme to plunder Spanish-American towns on the Pacific coast at a time when England was at peace with Spain. Few Englishmen even whispered the word "piracy" when Drake returned with a treasure estimated to be as great as £2,500,000. Despite Spanish clamors that "El Draque" be hanged, Elizabeth went aboard his *Golden Hind* and knighted her bold corsair. This was, in a sense, a sanction of successful piracy, and gave credence to a later observation by Sir Walter Raleigh: "Did you ever know of any that were pirates for millions? They only that work for small things are pirates."

It was alleged that a pirate by the name of Fleming was the first to report the appearance of the Spanish Armada in the English Channel, and certainly the presence of so many ex-pirates in the crews of the Royal Navy played an important role in the defeat of the enemy. Yet the decline of piracy in the Channel dates from the defeat of the Armada. The subsequent war with Spain removed the source of the pirates' plunder, for treasure ships do not sail in hostile seas. But if a seaman could dodge the naval press gangs, he could satisfy the demands of both patriotism and lucrative employment by shipping aboard a privateer.

The accession of James I brought an end to the war between England

and Spain and unemployment to many whose only trade was the sea. Men-of-war were laid up, crews discharged, and the merchant fleet was unable to absorb the sudden increase in unemployed seamen, even when some became so desperate that they offered to sail for food alone. In searching for work ashore, they were forced to compete for the few available jobs with men from the recently disbanded army. Captain John Smith explained why so many sought relief in piracy:

King James, who from his infancie had reigned in peace with all Nations, had no imployment for those men of warre so that those that were rich rested with that they had; those that were poore and had nothing but from hand to mouth, turned Pirats; some, because they became sleighted of those for whom they had got much wealth; some, for that they could not get their due; some, that had lived bravely, would not abase themselves to poverty; some vainly, only to get a name; others for revenge, covetousnesse, or as ill.

Ex-heroes turned pirate to prey not only on foreign commerce, but on the shipping of the nation that had used them in a time of crisis and had then tossed them aside with so little concern for their future. English trade was crippled and fell off. Armed ships sent out to run them down usually released captured pirates after relieving them of their booty. Even those who were brought in were not punished to the full extent of the law, if at all. Although English ports were generally closed to them, the pirates found it possible to put into ports in the south of Ireland for repairs and supplies. And for the next hundred years there were few pirate crews that did not include a substantial number of Irishmen.

To add to the distress of merchant shipping in the Channel, Barbary corsairs began to plunder in these narrow seas, so much so that Sir Henry Mainwaring was sent out to clear English waters of all freebooters. This was an instance of sending out a pirate to catch a pirate, for Mainwaring had been one of the most noted of freebooters until pardoned by the Crown. He still acted more like a pirate than an agent of the government, and did not confine his activities to the Channel. He sailed to the Grand Banks off Newfoundland ostensibly to recruit men, but seized the occasion to plunder the French and Portuguese fishing vessels he found there. Yet Mainwaring's exploits as a pirate chaser were so notable that his became one of the most feared names on the seas.

Although James I frowned upon attacks on English or even Spanish ships, he held few reservations if the victims were non-Christian or "infidels." He invested in piratical expeditions to the Red Sea, and always took for his treasury a percentage of the plunder. His son and successor, Charles I, actually granted commissions for such expeditions, and pirate ships were allowed, even ordered, to fly the colors of the Royal Navy. The profits from a single voyage to the Red Sea were sometimes estimated to be as high as £30,000.

Piracy in home waters still fluctuated with the strength of the Royal Navy, but usually gained in periods immediately following wars. The focus of operations was also beginning to shift; European pirates were voyaging more toward the Near East, while in the Caribbean a new breed of freebooter was gaining strength—the buccaneer.

Spain, because of her early voyages of discovery, had gained a strong foothold in the New World and jealously guarded the treasure-trove that had made her one of the great nations of Europe. Richard Hakluyt, the great chronicler of exploration and discovery, observed that "Whoever is conversant with the Portugal and Spanish writers, shall find that they account all other nations for pirates, rovers, and thieves, which visit any heathen coast that they have sailed by or looked on." And, in general, the West Indies were thought of as Spanish possessions and were so respected for many years; but Spanish ships, homeward bound and laden with the treasures of the west, were considered fair game.

Buccaneers and pirates were able to operate freely in the New World as a result of the defeat of the Spanish Armada, for with the destruction of Spain's sea power went her monopoly of the Americas. Although she was able to maintain a hold on most of her possessions in what was known as Spanish America, she was unable to prevent colonization or trade in areas not yet settled. Yet Spain made efforts to maintain her North American claims, especially when there were threats to the Bahama Channel off the coast of Florida, the homeward route of her treasure galleons. In 1562 when the French under Jean Ribaut attempted to settle in Florida, the alien colonists were either massacred or sent to the galleys. And in December, 1604, the Venetian ambassador in London reported that the Spanish had captured two English vessels in the West Indies and, claiming them to be pirates, had "cut off the hands, feet, noses and ears of the crews and smeared them with honey, and tied them to the trees to be tortured by flies and other insects."

Still, the rewards were too promising for bold adventurers to be frightened away by Spanish atrocities. Other European nations began to secure footholds in the Americas. Although colonization ventures often attracted men of courage and ambition, there were likewise inducements for many who could be characterized only as the scum and off-scourings of mankind. If a point may be stretched, the practice of buccaneering may be said to have come out of patriotic impulses. Yet, apart from patriotism, buccaneers were usually a surly, savage, and filthy lot.

The earliest of the buccaneers in the West Indies seem to have been French political and religious refugees who had somehow made their way out to the islands. A rather substantial number wandered to the western portion of Hispaniola (present day Haïti). The area had been previously colonized by Spain, but most of the Spaniards had left the island for the greater fortunes of the continent, especially after the conquests of Mexico and Peru. The cattle and swine they left behind had thrived and multiplied. French refugees straggled in, most of whom went native, living off the land with the sky as their roof in almost as wild a state as the livestock they found there.

These people eked out a primitive existence by drying and salting meat "after the Indian fashion." Long strips of meat were smoked and dried over "boucans," a grating made of green sticks. This not only preserved the meat, but made it tasty enough to excite the palates of mariners long accustomed to a diet of salt pork. Because of this method of curing flesh, these people gradually gained the name of "boucaniers," "bucaniers" or "buccaneers." They had few firearms with which to defend themselves, but there was little to fear, for the Indians had been almost exterminated by the Spanish. Their numbers grew as they were joined by deserters from passing ships, escaped indentured servants from Barbados, and refugees of nearly every nationality.

The dried meat of the buccaneers gained high repute among seafarers, who began to stop by Hispaniola to replenish their supply of meat. In an effort to secure muskets and ammunition for their hunting, the buccaneers began to trade hides, tallow, and dried meat to non-Spanish ships. As the buccaneer population grew, many felt crowded and about 1630 began to drift over to the uninhabited island of Tortuga, although it, too, was still claimed by Spain.

The Spanish raided Hispaniola in an attempt to eliminate the buccaneers. Those who were captured were summarily executed on the spot, and the cattle were slain in an effort to eliminate the supply of beef. Many additional buccaneers fled to Tortuga (now called Île de la Tortue).

Spain was to regret this move, for the buccaneers, unable to subsist on the land, took to the sea. Sailing in crudely constructed native dugouts, they attacked and captured small Spanish ships, and with these they took larger ships in which to roam the Caribbean. The English term for these sea-rovers was freebooters, which the French translated as *flibustiers,* and which the English took back again as filibuster. In any language, the proper term was pirate. The Spanish, through their efforts to eliminate an irritant, had "converted butchers of cattle into butchers of men."

As the buccaneers were driven from Hispaniola, the population of Tortuga swelled. This turtle-shaped island was but a few leagues northwest of Hispaniola. The complexion of the population gradually changed as the buccaneers were joined by sailors who jumped ship, while many of the original group tired of their haphazard existence and returned to Europe. Some say that those of the original group who occupied themselves in hunting were termed buccaneers, while those who sailed out on plundering expeditions were called filibusters. The English seem to have been the persons who began to use buccaneer as a synonym for pirate, while the Dutch preferred the phrase, "zee rovers."

From about 1630, and for the next eighty years despite Spanish efforts

A dugout canoe from Haiti similar to those used by the buccaneers.

to dislodge them, the people of Tortuga lived in something akin to a pirate "republic." They banded together into a loose organization they styled the "Confederacy of the Brethren of the Coast." Tortuga was fortified with captured Spanish guns, and the coast was defended with captured Spanish ships. Piracy had become so profitable that the majority of the buccaneers no longer wasted their time in drying meat over boucans. The island became a great storehouse for plunder taken from the Spanish which was, in turn, bartered for spirits, guns, gunpowder, and other necessaries and luxuries from the Dutch and French ships that now made Tortuga a regular port of call. This avenue to wealth attracted other adventurers, and the buccaneers changed from a basically timid people to a boisterous group, spending their money on great quantities of brandy which "they drink as liberally as the Spaniards do clear fountain water."

The French were the first to come to the conclusion that Tortuga might serve as a useful base. In 1640 a Monsieur Levasseur of Saint Christopher, with a company of fifty other Frenchmen, made a surprise attack on Tortuga and took possession of the island, with Levasseur establishing himself as governor. The fort he constructed was strong enough to drive off one Spanish fleet that made an attack on the place. The new governor ruled with wisdom and without too much interference insofar as the buccaneers were concerned, and the island prospered under Levasseur.

Buccaneers seldom went far out to sea in the early days. Operating from small boats, powered either by oars or by a sail or two, they lurked in the creeks and along the coast to surprise smaller Spanish vessels. Yet as early as 1654 buccaneers, traveling in canoes, had plundered the Mosquito Coast of Nicaragua. Not until around 1665 did these people embark on piracy in a traditional fashion. A buccaneer of French origin by the name of Pierre le Grand was the first real pirate leader of note in these waters. In a small ship, moved by both oars and sail, manned by twenty-eight men, Le Grand attacked a much larger vessel commanded by a vice-admiral of the Spanish fleet. Before attacking at dusk, Le Grand ordered his surgeon to bore a hole in the bottom of his own vessel to eliminate any thoughts of retreat. The surprise was complete, so much so that the Spanish were led to cry out: "Jesus bless us! Are these devils, or what are they?" The plunder was good and the share-out generous. Pierre le Grand and several of his crew decided to return immediately to France to live out their days in genteel retirement. His venture lost nothing in the telling and others were tempted to follow the trail that he had blazed.

Adventurers of all nationalities began to drift into Tortuga. France issued letters of marque authorizing privateering mariners of all nationalities to prey on Spanish shipping in the Caribbean, although those two nations were not officially at war. Basically, the French were attempting to reduce Spain's potential as an enemy when the anticipated war did break out between the two nations. More important, there was the personal motive involved; all governors who issued commissions were entitled to one tenth of the plunder.

Desperate men gained notoriety, although not fame that endeared them to their fellow human beings. There was, for instance, the terrible François Lolonois, who boasted that he never spared a prisoner's life, and who gained a fortune by sacking the city of Maracaibo on the Venezuelan coast. Lewis Scott, an Englishman, pillaged Campeche on the Yucatan peninsula. Others who won fame and fortune on the Spanish Main bore such names as Pierre François, Roche Brasiliano, John Davis, Bartholomew the Portuguese, and Montbars the Exterminator.

The infamous Francis Lolonois (*left*) and Roche Brasiliano, who gained fortune and notoriety on the Spanish Main.

Lolonois cuts the heart from one victim to feed to another captive.

The Spanish made a number of attempts to wipe out the pirates on Tortuga, but the latter always returned. Yet this harassment was successful to the extent that many of the buccaneers began to look for a place where they would not be subjected to such periodic irritations. Some years earlier, an expedition under Colonel Venables and Admiral Penn had been dispatched to Hispaniola to take that island as a base from which English shipping might be protected. They had failed miserably. But in 1665 they had fallen on and taken the Spanish island of Jamaica, which few people seemed to care about. At the end of a narrow spit of land stood Cagua, a little town that fitted perfectly into the pirate scheme of things.

Jamaica, whose first governor was authorized to issue privateering commissions, became even more of a pirate's haven than had Tortuga. Port Royal, as Cagua was renamed, with pirate gold and plunder flowing into it became one of the richest towns in the hemisphere and undoubtedly earned its reputation as the "wickedest city in the world." Yet it was through its large population of transient fighting seamen that the British were able to retain Jamaica. As late as 1774, Edward Long, historian of Jamaica, was to write, "It is to the buccaneers that we owe possession of Jamaica to this hour." Not only the pirates, but the British Navy, operated out of this port to plunder Spanish colonial towns. On one occasion, the navy and the buccaneers (with privateering commissions) made a combined attack on Santiago, Cuba. And after every war, declared or undeclared, when there was a shift in foreign policy and the governors' right to issue letters of marque was restricted, the buccaneers resorted to outright piracy.

One of the most famous of the buccaneers operating out of Jamaica was Sir Henry Morgan. People still dispute whether Morgan was a true member of the pirate clan, but none can deny that when sacking a town he proved as cruel as the most ruthless buccaneer. His rise to fame, strangely enough, came about as the result of a treaty between England and Spain in May, 1667. In this document, each country agreed not to interfere with the other's trade. But the wording was vague, and both nations interpreted the document to suit their own purposes. The West Indies and America were not specifically mentioned; Spain assumed English possessions in these areas to be fair game. Britain, on the other hand, supposing these places were included, sent instructions to Sir

Thomas Modyford, governor of Jamaica, to recall all privateering commissions.

Modyford had received disturbing information that the Spanish in Cuba were assembling a fleet for a strike against Jamaica. The island's only defense was the buccaneers, and Modyford had no money to pay them with. They would not be persuaded to fight unless they were at least given a prospect of plunder. There was also the danger that Jamaica might lose the services of the buccaneers altogether because the French governor of Tortuga was freely issuing commissions against both the English and the Spanish. Helpless, the Council of Jamaica unanimously resolved to grant a special commission to "Colonel" Henry Morgan, allowing him to attack Spanish shipping.

Henry Morgan sailed with 700 men (both English and French) in twelve ships. They overwhelmed the inland city of Puerto del Principe in Cuba, plundering the inhabitants, and would have burnt the town had not the populace ransomed their homes with 1,000 beeves. Still, the men were unhappy because the city had not furnished the booty they had been led to expect. Morgan persuaded them to continue with him for an assault on Porto Bello, the city on the east coast of Panama, through which all the treasure from Peru passed. Although the city was defended by three strong forts, it was not enough to hold against the fury of the buccaneers. The last fort was captured as Morgan's men used captured monks and nuns, many of whom were shot down, as living shields as they brought up scaling ladders. With the fall of the city they acted in typical buccaneer fashion, looting the town (even the churches), raping the women, and torturing prisoners (including small children) to make them reveal where valuables had been hidden. After routing a Spanish relief expedition and holding the town for thirty-one days, Morgan and his men sailed back to Jamaica.

Although he had been authorized to attack Spanish shipping only, Morgan received no more than a mild reproof from Modyford for plundering the towns. He was allowed to retain his commission. The governor's reasoning, which seems logical, was that the attacks on the Spanish towns greatly reduced the danger of an invasion of Jamaica in that the enemy were forced to keep their military forces at home to defend their cities. After successful expeditions against Maracaibo and

The sacking of Puerto del Principe in Cuba by Henry Morgan and his buccaneers.

Gibraltar in Venezuela, in which a New England ship of thirty guns played a part, Modyford, at the insistence of the Crown, withdrew Morgan's commission. For the time being, Morgan seemingly retired to the uneventful life of a planter.

In 1670, the Spanish renewed their attacks on Jamaica. Several coastal villages were sacked and burned. Morgan came out of retirement. He and his buccaneers were given commissions of great latitude—in fact, he was given license to do almost anything he wished. Modyford, in issuing such a commission, was deliberately flouting instructions from London, but he felt that the employment of the buccaneers was the best possible defensive expedient for a government with an empty treasury. French buccaneers from Hispaniola and Tortuga flocked in to join Morgan as he gathered a fleet of thirty-six ships manned by 2,000 men.

Henry Morgan was once again blessed with that fabulous success that had been associated with his name in the past. Taking over the island of Old Providence for use as a base, his buccaneers overran the town of Chagres on the east coast of Panama. Then, after a jungle march and a short, fierce fight, they took the city of Panama on the Pacific coast, reputedly the richest town in Spanish America. As Morgan was "a man little given to mercy," there was the usual murder, torture, and rape before the town was burned to the ground, either by the Spanish or the buccaneers. It has been estimated that 175 mules were required to carry the booty, along with 600 prisoners to be ransomed, when the pirates marched away towards the Atlantic. A riotous welcome awaited them at Port Royal, for the buccaneers had so sorely crippled the Spanish that the latter had abandoned all plans to invade Jamaica.

When Spanish war vessels were sent out to sweep the freebooters from the seas, the buccaneers, by the very simplicity of their tactics, usually succeeded in destroying the enemy. The Spaniards, trained in formal naval warfare, seemed to expect their adversaries to follow accepted precepts and maneuvers. The buccaneers, however, resorting to cunning and ingenuity, usually managed to outwit the navy. But the carefree existence of the buccaneers was drawing to an end.

After Morgan had sailed on his expedition to Panama, the so-called "Treaty of America" reached Jamaica. This was in itself a by-product of Morgan's past successes and an attempt to correct the misunderstandings arising out of the treaty of 1667. Under this document, Spain, for the first time, recognized British rights to trade and colonize in the New World. The result was a new British policy of appeasement toward Spain. In reply to Spanish complaints, a new governor was sent out to Jamaica with orders for Modyford to be returned home under arrest. Six months later, Morgan was summoned to London "to answer for his offences against the King, his crown and dignity."

Yet neither Morgan nor Modyford suffered punishment, perhaps because of the shares of plunder received by the King and his brother, the Duke of York. It is to be suspected that no judge or jury would dare convict so popular a hero; indeed, both men were rewarded for their past transgressions. Modyford was returned to Jamaica as chief justice, while Morgan was knighted and made lieutenant governor of that island under Lord John Vaughan. In that official position, Morgan hanged without remorse some of his former comrades of the sea who were so unfortunate as to be captured while practicing their old trade.

The great days of the buccaneers were now over. They had so completely diminished the possibility of a Spanish thrust that they were no longer needed as an auxiliary force to defend Jamaica. Planters, whose labor force in the past had run off to join the buccaneers, welcomed the Treaty of America and urged that its provisions be upheld. The suppression of the buccaneers likewise meant that trading ships of all nations would now visit the island with greater frequency, no longer fearing molestation by sea rovers. And there was the persistent fear that if the buccaneers were allowed to continue their operations out of Port Royal, Spain would most certainly seek reprisals.

Few of the buccaneers took advantage of Governor Vaughan's offer of pardon and amnesty, although some did accept and used their share of the plunder to establish themselves as planters. The majority, however, having spent their shares almost as soon as they received them, returned to the most rewarding trade they knew.

Since there were no longer opportunities to plunder the Spanish colonies, some secured privateering commissions from the governors of French and Danish islands, while others cast aside all pretenses and turned pirate, even though it meant outlawry. There wasn't too much to distinguish between the two groups other than a scrap of paper, which neither

England nor Spain honored. Operations were now on a much smaller scale, for no longer was there a Morgan to build up a buccaneer fleet. Each ship ventured forth alone, and its operations generally were confined to the sea. Prizes were more difficult to take as the Spanish began to convoy their treasure ships with men-of-war. On the other hand, the pirates held few qualms about taking a British ship; in fact, so many were taken that Governor Thomas Lynch was led to complain that "This cursed trade has been so long followed, and there is so many of it that like weeds or hydras they spring up as fast as we can cut them down." Although there were no naval vessels to hunt down pirates, Lynch initiated a vigorous campaign against these outlaws of the sea, and the citizens of Port Royal soon became accustomed to the sight of the bodies of British pirates swinging in the breezes below the arm of the gibbet.

Morgan, on two occasions, was acting governor. He proved more ruthless than his predecessors, using all of his knowledge and cunning to entrap pirates. Terming his former followers "a dangerous pestilence" and "ravenous vermin" who had "now grown to the hight of Insolence," he hanged them high whenever they were so unfortunate as to fall into his hands. Some English buccaneers transferred their operations to the Pacific ocean. Those who left and those who were hanged were but a fraction of the pirates still active: such men as William Dampier, John Coxen, Richard Sawkins, Bartholomew Sharp and John Watling prowled the seas, some occasionally plundering Spanish coastal towns.

Times were better in 1683 when war broke out between France and Spain and letters of marque were once more easily obtainable from either country. Sometimes they even went so far as to hand out blank commissions which could be filled in by the holder. Although Jamaica was now almost completely closed as a place where English commissions could be had, Robert Clarke, the governor of the Bahamas, could usually be relied upon to issue them without asking too many questions. In general, commissions were not that important, especially if the holders were captured by the Spanish. Spanish governors made a practice of hanging privateers with their commissions tied around their necks. Still the documents proved useful in friendly or neutral ports and lent an air of respectability to piratical operations.

Because of the tolerant atmosphere, pirates began to drift into the

Bahamas. These islands were particularly well suited for those who pursued careers as pirates. This nest of islands, cays, and reefs of all shapes and sizes provided a reasonably safe haven for both pirates and privateers. More and more, the island of New Providence became a pirate rendez-vous.

In 1688, with war impending between England and France, a general pardon was proclaimed by the Crown. Many pirates came in to receive the royal clemency, and just as many, when war broke out again in 1689, went back to sea as privateers. It was this war—"King William's War," as it was termed in the English colonies—that finally eliminated the remnants of the "Brethren of the Coast." The bond of unity that had kept the English and French together in schemes of aggression against the common enemy, Spain, was now broken as these former allies could not help but take sides.

With the Treaty of Ryswick in 1697, the buccaneers became dormant, with many returning to Europe while others settled down in the islands as respectable businessmen and planters. Those who persisted in pursuing their former calling were pirates, pure and simple, who operated without semiofficial sanction of any kind. They looked for new hunting grounds and found them in two widely separated areas, the eastern seas and the North American coast.

Yet so long as fighting continued in Europe, as it did until 1713, with but brief breathing spells between wars, there were privateers in the New World. John Graves, collector of the customs for the Bahamas, noted in 1706, "War is no sooner ended but the West Indies always swarm with pirates." During Queen Anne's War (1702–1713), privateering had become particularly profitable in that an act of 1708 had allowed the owners and crews of privateers to share in the whole of the plunder without having to divert a share to the Crown. When peace so abruptly shut off income, thousands of seamen in the islands suddenly found themselves unemployed, and jobs were scarce aboard the merchantmen, even had they wanted to return to such drudgery. The numbers of the unemployed were swelled by those ex-convicts who had been transported to the colonies as indentured servants and having served their terms, or escaped from their masters, were now seeking a way of survival.

Many were loath to leave the Caribbean, that corner of the world that had held so much for them in the past. Then, too, for those who sought the pirate life, the islands provided safe anchorages and refuges with easy access to water and provisions. There was a need for a permanent base of operations. They found it on the proprietary island of New Providence in the Bahamas. These sparsely settled islands, in general, were too lean in natural resources to attract a regular trade, and pirates were welcomed by the inhabitants as an additional source of income. There were no objections from Governor Nicholas Trott, whose official income amounted to about thirty pounds a year. When Trott was eventually deposed for his dealings with the pirates, it was said of Colonel Webb, his successor, "If he were to give an account of how he made £8,000 in two years in such a paltry island, I believe he would [say] he but trod in the steps of his predecessor, Trott, the greatest pirate-broker that ever was in America."

After Nassau, the chief town of New Providence, was destroyed and plundered by the Spanish and French in 1703, many of the inhabitants fled the island. Government disintegrated, and the Lords Proprietors (essentially the same as those who held Carolina) appeared to lose interest in promoting their welfare. In 1714, with no particularly strong authority in the Bahamas, it was only natural that the pirates move in and take over. A better pirate harbor could not have been found; it was large enough to accommodate as many as 500 pirate vessels, yet it was too shallow for large men-of-war. Provisions were available in sufficient quantity. Nassau, according to the governor of Bermuda, soon became a "sink or nest of infamous rascals."

The pirates also attracted a more respectable group of individuals to the islands—merchants and traders who purchased the plunder at cheap prices and then smuggled the goods over into the mainland colonies. Where there was money to be made, there was growth. Stores, taverns, and brothels, often of crude palm-thatched construction, began to line the streets of Nassau.

As the competition for prizes increased in the Caribbean, nearly all nations were forced to resort to the convoy system, and a number of the West Indian pirates turned their attention to the North American mainland. Still, so many remained in the islands that the governor of the Leeward Islands complained that he could not travel from one island to another without fear of interception by these sea rovers.

The commanders of naval vessels stationed in the islands were of little help. They were not responsible to the governors and refused to receive their orders. Some turned to the legal, and profitable, exercise of hiring their vessels out for convoy duty. So desperate was the situation that some merchants agreed to pay as much as twelve and one half per cent of the value of their cargoes for the privilege of a naval escort. As a result, many captains of the Royal Navy were reluctant to eliminate a source of income by destroying the pirates. When freight rates became excessive, these same naval commanders offered to carry cargoes in men-of-war at a cheaper rate than that of ordinary merchant vessels. Others hired sloops for personal trading ventures, arming them with naval guns and manning them with naval personnel. These last practices were illegal, but the captains were far enough removed from authority to become a law unto themselves, and it became "impossible to bear their haughty airs and insulting ways." The government's answer to the complaints of the island governors was to send out more naval vessels whose commanders learned fast and promptly joined in the game.

In response to repeated demands by the governors of the West Indian islands, the Board of Trade suggested that a new governor of the Bahamas be appointed by the Crown rather than by the Lords Proprietors as in the past. One logical candidate was Woodes Rogers, an adventurer who should be better known. In 1708 Rogers had sailed around the world in command of a privateer, returning to England with £800,000 worth of Spanish treasure. He also brought back a marooned sailor from Juan Fernandez Island, one Alexander Selkirk, who was later to be immortalized as Daniel Defoe's Robinson Crusoe. In the autumn of 1717, Rogers was able to lease the Bahamas for twenty-one years from the Lords Proprietors and to secure a commission from the Crown as "Captain-General and Governor-in-Chief in and over our Bahama Islands in America." His authority included the power to suppress piracy by any means whatsoever.

By this time influential London merchants whose normal trade patterns were being disrupted by the pirates petitioned George I to do something about the situation. But the King, in an effort to protect his little Electorate of Hanover against the threats of Charles XII of Sweden, concentrated the British fleet in the Baltic. No additional ships for use as pirate-chasers could be spared for the Caribbean.

To partially ease the situation, a royal proclamation promised amnesty for all piracies committed before January 5, 1718, if the pirates came and surrendered themselves to the authorities by September 5 of that same year. A large number took advantage of the opportunity to come in, some of whom were enlisted in a force designed to repel a Spanish threat. Others, led by Charles Vane and Edward Teach, resented what they felt was an infringement on the rights of pirates and disliked the prospect of a settled and stable government. Many of these disgruntled freebooters sailed for the mainland colonies. Rogers reacted with characteristic vigor and, in December, 1718, hanged ten pirates on his own responsibility, "fully satisfied that we have not erred in justice." Captain Benjamin Hornigold, a former ringleader among pirates, after taking an oath, was sent out in a sloop with a crew of former pirates to clear the seas of the other blackguards. Although there is a suggestion that Hornigold and his crew may have engaged in a bit of piracy now and then, when there was no prospect of getting caught, he ostensibly chased pirates until he perished in a shipwreck.

Although piracy continued in the West Indies, and would for many a year, it declined in influence since pirates no longer had a base from which to operate. Those who remained continued clandestine operations with sympathizers ashore. The islanders seldom reported them for "their consciences were so tender, that they wou'd not have the blood of a man to lye at their door; besides it was to be fear'd that this . . . would make our vessels fare the worse for it, when they happened to fall into the pyrates hands." Some sailed for other uninhabited and isolated islands, while others found a friend in the Danish governor at St. Thomas in the Virgin Islands. Many began to operate off the southern mainland colonies, notably off Charleston and the Capes of Virginia. By this time the basic pattern of piracy had taken shape; practices that had taken form under earlier corsairs and among the buccaneers now had many of the rough edges worn away. It might almost be said that pirates operated under an unwritten constitution.

II

GENTRY OF THE BLACK
FLAG

*"Plenty and Satiety, Pleasure and Ease, Liberty
and Power."*

Pirates were a sorry lot of human trash. Much whimsical romanticism
has created a quixotic image from rogues and knaves. It didn't take
much to make a pirate—an evil spirit in a restless body. Life was a fleeting
thing with pirates and they held it cheap—both their own and that of
their victims—but they were determined to live for the present and allow
the morrow to take care of itself. To the average pirate, life was either a
lark or a treadmill along the path of eternity.

It wasn't difficult for a man to become a pirate once he had made his
choice and "reduced himself afresh to the savage state of nature by
declaring war against all mankind. . . ." All he need do was to find
companions of a similar bent; this was no difficult task in the seventeenth
and eighteenth centuries. A merchant seaman lived a brutal life. Discipline was as cruel as it was necessary. Food was poor and often crawling
with weevils. Wages were low and the voyages long. Life as a pirate, on
the other hand, promised adventure, gold, and a good life, although
perhaps a short one. Even then, the hazards were no greater than those of
any other occupation on the sea. A pirate career was attractive enough to
lessen the fear of the hangman's noose, but even in periods of great

piratical activity, the number of pirates captured and executed was negligible in contrast to the total number engaged.

Privateering, of course, was one of the most influential factors in the increase of pirating. Men who had become accustomed to the free and easy life in time of war found it difficult to adjust to the humdrum existence of a world at peace. The transition from legal booty to illegal plunder was simpler, for it involved no great changes in habits or mental attitudes. In fact, many pirates continued to refer to themselves as "privateers," although sailing under the Jolly Roger. Their status was determined by the diplomats who made the peace.

The risk was not so great when it is considered that a single voyage in a pirate ship might gain a man a greater fortune than a lifetime of honest toil. In the minds of many pirates, theirs was a Robin Hood sort of existence; they robbed from the rich and gave to the poor. But they were the poor. The articles they signed lent a democratic air to the enterprise and cast the officers and men into a partnership.

Captain John Smith once observed that the low wages paid ordinary seamen forced them to steal, "and when they are once entered into that trade, they are hardly reclaimed." Perhaps the best expression of why men went "a-pyrating," was in a statement by the infamous Bartholomew Roberts:

In an honest Service there is thin Commons, low Wages and hard Labour; in this Plenty and Satiety, Pleasure and Ease, Liberty and Power. and who would not ballance Creditor on this Side when all the Hazard that is run for it, at worst, is only a forelock or two at choaking.

The three great sources of pirates were merchant ships, the Royal Navy, and privateers, supplemented by seamen who joined the company from the crew of a captured vessel. In the Royal Navy, the desertion rate was such that crewmen were seldom allowed shore leave during wartime. Discipline aboard His Majesty's ships was maintained through a liberal administration of the lash. Prize money, in comparison with that shared by the crew of privateers, was scarce, for the navy concentrated on enemy men-of-war rather than merchant shipping. Even when there was prize money, the ordinary seamen were often cheated out of their just shares by the officers.

Bartholomew Roberts, who ravaged shipping off the coasts of North America and South America from Newfoundland to the Caribbean Sea. An engraving from the original edition of Johnson, *A General History of the Pirates,* 1724.

In the colonies, escaped indentured servants, and even runaway slaves, were often willing to seek new identities aboard a pirate ship. But the average pirate sailing in North American waters claimed England as his home. For instance, of the twenty-four men of Captain John Quelch's crew tried and convicted in Boston in 1704, there were thirteen Englishmen, four Irishmen, two Scots, one Swiss, one Dutchman, and three New Englanders. Most of them had a seafaring background, but listed among this group were a cooper, a blacksmith, a goldsmith, a merchant, and a tanner. Perhaps the strangest pirate of all, or so it was claimed by Horace Walpole, was one Lancelot Blackburne, who went out to the West Indies in 1681, joined the buccaneers, and later, after his return to England, became Archbishop of York.

A surprising number of Negroes and mulattoes were listed among the members of pirate crews; some were runaway slaves while others were free men. In some companies, as many as one-sixth of the total number of pirates were Negroes. In 1721 there was a report that fifty Negroes, under the command of a white man, had run away from the French island of Martinique to seek a career in piracy. Captured Negro pirates were usually hanged along with their white comrades, but occasionally they were sold into slavery.

The pirate philosophy was perhaps best expressed by Captain Charles Bellamy, who prided himself for his flowery oratory, when he berated the captain of a captured merchantman who refused to join the pirate crew:

Damn ye, you are a sneaking puppy, and so are all those who submit to be governed by laws which rich men have made for their own security, for the cowardly whelps have not the courage otherwise to defend what they get by their own knavery. Damn them for a set of crafty rascals, and you who serve them for a parcel of hen-hearted numbskulls. They villify us, the scoundrels do, when there is only this difference: they rob the poor under the cover of the law, forsooth, and we plunder the rich under the protection of our own courage. Had you not better make one of us, than sneak after the arses of those villains for employment?

You are a devilish conscious rascal, damn ye! I am a free prince and have as much authority to make war on the whole world as he who has a hundred sail of ships and an army of a hundred thousand men in the field. And this my conscience tells me; but there is no arguing with such sniveling puppies who allow superiors to kick them about the deck at pleasure, and pin their faith upon the pimp of a parson, a squab who neither practises or believes what he puts upon the chuckle-headed fools he preaches to.

"Going on the account" was the term used when a man embarked on a piratical career. Translated loosely, this simply meant "No prey, no pay." In other words, every member of every pirate crew was a shareholder in the company. They owned their ship, and they elected those under whom they were to serve.

Once a man took up the pirate life, it was not uncommon that he change his name, especially if his family reputation fell within the realm of respectability. Often he preferred a nickname that had been bestowed on him by his shipmates, hence, "Blackbeard," "Gentleman Harry," "Calico Jack," "Long Ben," "Montbars the Exterminator," "Roche Brasiliano," "Half-Bottom" (the result of a physical condition caused by a cannon ball passing too near the seat of his pants), and "Captain Flogger."

Few, if any, pirate ships were ever built specifically for that purpose, but the acquisition of a vessel wasn't too difficult. Perhaps the easiest procedure was mutiny at sea, where the endless roll of the waves obliterated all evidence of murder. Ships were likewise exchanged with little or no expense. Many a pirate crew set out by stealing a likely looking vessel. Rowing out to an anchored ship in the dark of night, they would overwhelm those members of the crew still on board. Later, if they captured a more suitable craft they merely shifted their personal belongings and armament.

The typical pirate vessel was fairly small and fast. The sloop was felt to be ideal. Particularly suitable were the large, fast sailing sloops of Bermuda. The sails of this fore-and-aft rigged ship were easier to handle than those of a square-rigged vessel, especially when operating in shoal waters near the shore where maneuverability was essential. When a larger ship was used, one rigged as a brigantine was felt to be the most desirable. A shallow-draft ship was especially favored in that it enabled the crew to escape pursuit by fleeing into sounds and creeks where heavier men-of-war could not follow.

Considerable changes were made in a ship when it was converted to

Shipping in the York River off Yorktown, showing a sloop *(center)* common in the eighteenth century and particularly favored by pirates for its speed and sailing qualities.

A brigantine of the eighteenth century.

pirate use. Gunwales were raised, not only for greater protection in battle, but to provide concealment for the crew when approaching a prize. All deckhouses were usually razed to leave the deck flush, which not only presented a low silhouette against the horizon, but lessened the danger from flying splinters. A ship so cut down was sometimes termed "clean tailored." In times of battle, the hammocks of the crew were lashed along the gunwales as an added protection against small arms fire. Other renovations were made below decks, primarily for the accommodation of the crew. Pirate crews were large; there was seldom enough space below for the entire company, and some were forced to sleep out on deck, even in periods of storm.

One definite advantage of a small ship was that it was easier to careen. All ships had to be periodically careened to remove the marine encrustations below the water line lest the speed of the vessel be too greatly reduced. When pressed for time, pirates oft-times resorted to an expedient known as "boot-topping" by anchoring in shallow waters, moving the guns and other equipment to one side of the ship to create as great a list as possible and scraping off as much of the sea junk as they could reach below the water line. They then repeated the operation for the other side. At best, however, this was but a temporary measure until a proper careening could be made.

A good careening shore was usually a shallow and secluded cove, with trees growing almost to the water's edge. The ship was brought in close to the beach, the topmasts removed, and the guns and other equipment shifted to land. Block and tackle, fastened from the masts to the trees, pulled the ship over until she lay almost on her side. After the marine life was scraped from the hull and the necessary repairs and caulking completed, the bottom was coated with tar, sulphur, and tallow. Then the ship was pulled over to the other side and the operation repeated. In the topics, because of the prevalence of the teredo worm, ships had to be careened as often as three times each year. While this operation was in progress, a portion of the crew mounted the guns in hastily constructed earthworks overlooking the beach.

There was little consistency in the names that pirates gave their ships, although one of their favorites seems to have been *Revenge*. The significance of this seems to have been lost in time, but one would suspect that the pirates felt it necessary to express their resentment against a society that had treated them so shabbily in the past. The extreme of this liking for the name was Captain Richard Worley's *New York Revenge's Revenge*. Their adventurous existence was sometimes reflected in the names the pirates bestowed on their ships: *Defiance, Adventure, Black Joke, Bravo, Sudden Death, Flying Horse, Snap Dragon, Welfare, Batchelor's Delight, Good Fortune, Night Rambler, Scowerer, Flying Dragon*, and the *Jolly Shark*. Some, like Stede Bonnet's *Royal James* or John Quelch's *Charles II* suggested political implications. Many ironic names were given to pirate ships, including such poetic or religious allusions as the *Prophet Daniel, Happy Delivery, Most Holy Trinity, Blessings, Mayflower, Liberty, Childhood, Amity, Merry Christmas, Morning Star, Peace*, and *Black Angel*.

Service in merchant ships or the men-of-war of the Royal Navy had led the average seaman to fear and despise discipline. This rebellion against eighteenth-century order led to a practice of democracy that bordered on anarchy. Inasmuch as the ship usually belonged to the crew and had been acquired by their joint effort, there was no officer who could claim absolute authority over the men. The average pirate feared placing too much authority in the hands of any one man. They elected their captains and could depose them if they felt it necessary. On occasion, if the vote for the captain was almost equally divided, the crew split into two different

groups, each going its own way. Daniel Defoe noted that on one pirate
ship there were thirteen captains elected over the span of a few months.
The stereotyped picture of pirate captains as seagoing dictators who
exercised extreme tyranny to maintain discipline was seldom true. A
captain could be removed too easily not to court the respect and affection
of his crew.

The customary reason for deposing a captain was incompetence or
failure to gain booty. The pirate captain held no authority except in
action. According to one contemporary, "The Captain's power is uncon-
trollable in chase or in battle, drubbing, cutting or even shooting anyone
who does deny his command." Some captains used a trumpet to signal
their men during the clash of battle. Once the fight was over, however,
the captain was not allowed to issue an order to any member of the crew.
Although he was given custody of the prisoners, he was not allowed to
decide their fate, for "all business of this nature, must be done in public
and by a majority of votes by the whole company."

Although the captain was given a greater share of the plunder than any
other member of the crew, he had few real privileges. He was allowed a
cabin, but it could not be considered private. One late seventeenth-century
chronicler of piracy noted, "Every man may at his pleasure intrude into
the captain's cabin, swear at him, or take what part of his victuals or drink
that may please them without his offering to deny them." He ate the same
rations as the rest of the crew and was given the same portions. Yet, as in
every rule, there were inconsistencies. Many a captain, especially among
those who became better known, exercised greater command over the
men through their terror of him plus the fact that he gathered a coterie
about him to lend force to his orders.

Perhaps an even more important officer than the captain was the
quartermaster, likewise elected by the crew. It was his duty to lead the
boarding party aboard every ship attacked, and he was to command every
party detached in small boats and sent out on a dangerous enterprise. His
duties included the responsibility to decide what plunder was to be taken
from a prize, although all jewels, gold, and silver were automatically
seized. Selection of plunder was usually based on the space in the hold
and the availability of markets. Books were kept on the plunder taken,
and the quartermaster was responsible for it until there was a share-out,

which was customarily done, after a deduction for expenses, soon after the prize was captured.

Although more serious offenses were tried before a pirate jury, the quartermaster had the right to order punishments for such misdemeanors as quarreling, misuse of prisoners, or the neglect of arms. And, with the support of a majority of the crew, he was the only man on board who was allowed to administer a flogging. Should two members of the crew start a fight on board ship, it was the quartermaster's duty to attempt a reconciliation. If arbitration failed, he was to take them ashore to settle their dispute with "sword and pistol," until blood was let. When the ship was not in action, the quartermaster was in command, but during battle he was not allowed to issue orders.

The remaining officers on board were similar to those aboard a ship of the Royal Navy. Some were elected, but those posts requiring special talents were appointed by either the captain or the quartermaster. Occasionally a captain was allowed a lieutenant, but he held no authority whatsoever unless the captain was killed in action, whereupon he was to assume command at once.

One of the most important subordinate officers aboard a pirate vessel was the master, or sailing master. This "sea artist," as he was sometimes called, was responsible for navigating the ship and trimming the sails. The boatswain, or bo'sun, was accountable for the maintenance of the vessel and was in charge of all naval stores. The gunner took care of the ordinance and exercised the crew in its use and care. Others who ranked above the general run of pirates were the sailmaker, carpenter, and surgeon. These men could be dismissed from their positions by a vote of the company, but they seldom were—their talents were too hard to come by. Surgeons were ill-trained or totally lacking in any formal training. On occasion, the carpenter would be pressed into service as a surgeon, primarily because his tools might prove useful in amputations. It is not too surprising that many contemporary accounts refer to pirate crews as "gangs."

Piracy, in general, was strictly a province of the male, although some captains are known to have carried their wives or mistresses with them when they went to sea. Anne Bonny and Mary Read were actually members of pirate crews and were said to have been more bloodthirsty than many of their male companions.

Pirates operated under a document that had some similarity to a constitution. Before every voyage each crew drew up and signed articles, based on earlier regulations used by the buccaneers. They were sworn to on the Bible, along with the consumption of a goodly supply of rum. No two sets of articles were the same, although those drawn up by the crew of Captain John Phillips in 1723 may be considered typical:

1. Every man shall obey civil Command; the Captain shall have one full Share and a half in all prizes; the Master, Carpenter, Boatswain, and Gunner shall have one Share and a quarter.

2. If any Man shall offer to run away, or keep any Secret from the Company, he shall be marroon'd with one Bottle of Powder, one Bottle of Water, one small Arm, and Shot.

3. If any Man shall steal any Thing in the Company, or game, to the Value of a Piece of Eight, he shall be marroon'd or shot.

4. If at any Time we shall meet another Marrooner (that is Pyrate) that Man shall sign his Articles without the Consent of our Company, shall suffer such Punishment as the Captain and Company shall think fit.

5. That Man that shall strike another whilst these Articles are in force, shall receive Moses's Law (that is 40 stripes lacking one) on the bare Back.

6. That Man that shall snap his Arms, or smoak Tobacco in the Hold, without a Cap to his Pipe, or carry a Candle lighted without a Lanthorn, shall suffer the same Punishment as in the former Articles.

7. That Man that shall not keep his Arms clean, fit for an Engagement, or Neglect his Business, shall be cut off from his Share, and suffer such other Punishment as the Captain and the Company shall think fit.

8. If any Man shall lose a Joint in time of an Engagement, shall have 400 Pieces of Eight; if a limb 800.

9. If at any time you meet with a prudent Woman, that Man that offers to meddle with her, without her Consent, shall suffer present Death.

Article eight was a relic of the buccaneers who had a more elaborate insurance agreement, as did some pirates:

Loss of right arm...................... 600 pieces of eight, or six slaves.
Loss of left arm....................... 500 pieces of eight, or five slaves.
Loss of right leg...................... 500 pieces of eight, or five slaves.

Loss of left leg...................... 400 pieces of eight, or four slaves.
Loss of an eye........................ 100 pieces of eight, or one slave.
Loss of a finger...................... 100 pieces of eight, or one slave.

Pirates often spent some time in designing the flag under which they were to sail. A pirate flag did not fly constantly at the mast head, for to dispel suspicion a national ensign would be run up while approaching a prospective victim. Once contact was made the Jolly Roger would be run up. The buccaneers, who held legal or semi-legal commissions as privateers, sailed under the flag of the nation that had issued that document. And some, when calling on a prize to surrender, would run a blood red ensign up the shrouds, a not-too-subtle suggestion that if their demands did not meet with speedy compliance, no quarter would be given. Yet the practice of pirates of English origin flying a red flag may well have originated in a royal proclamation of July, 1694 which stated that privateers sailing under English commissions should fly, in addition to the national ensign, "a Red Jack with the Union Jack described in a Canton of the upper corner thereof next the staff," a fabric sometimes termed a "Budgee jack."

The popular name for the pirate flag was "Jolly Roger," although the origins of the name are obscure. The term was used as early as 1719 and possibly much earlier. There are several explanations, one of the most popular stating that it was the English corruption of "joli Rouge," the term used by the French buccaneers. Another possibility came out of the eastern seas where the chiefs of Cannonore, notorious pirates, held the title of Ali Raja, meaning "King of the Sea," which the English pronounced "Olly Roger." Also there have been speculations that the term came from the English word "roger," meaning a begging vagabond, while one canting dictionary of 1725 identifies the term "Old Roger" with the Devil.

The use of the skull-and-bones insignia was not peculiar to piracy; such a design had long been a symbol of death. One of the first recorded uses of the emblem was by a French pirate, Emanuel Wynne, who flew, in 1700, "a sable ensign with cross-bones, a death's head, and an hourglass."

The design of pirate flags differed with the fancies of the crew. Some portrayed entire skeletons, others had the skeletons holding swords, while

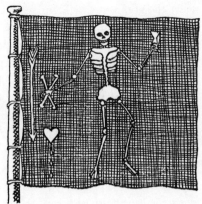

"The Flag had a Death in it, with an Hour Glass in one Hand, and cross-Bones in the other, a Dart by it, and underneath a Heart dropping three Drops of Blood." The flag of Bartholomew Roberts in 1722.

a favorite device was an hourglass, perhaps to signify to an intended victim that time was running out and he had best surrender while there was still an opportunity. Captain John Quelch was reported off the coast of Brazil in 1703, flying the "Old Roger," depicting "an anatomy with an hourglass in one hand and a dart in the heart with three drops of blood proceeding from it in the other." There are accounts of black skeletons on white flags, while one crew went so far as to letter their white flag with "For God and Liberty." Some made use of both red and black flags. With some crews, or captains, it became the practice to first run up the Jolly Roger, signifying an offer of quarter, and if this was not accepted and the victim chose to fight, the red flag was hoisted indicating that the offer had been withdrawn. But these gruesome bits of cloth were designed not so much to titillate the conceit of the crew as they were to strike terror into the hearts of the beholder.

There was always a near endless supply of recruits for pirate crews. The crew members of almost every prize were encouraged to sign the articles. Persuasion of a prospective member required little more than: "You have been serving a merchantman for twenty-five shillings a month. Here you may have seven or eight pounds a month if you can take it." Quite often there were volunteers in direct ratio to the cruelty of their former captain. Those who did volunteer were interviewed by the quartermaster, who explained the articles and who also had the authority to accept or reject the applicants. Seldom were prisoners "forced" against their wills, although sailing masters, carpenters, and surgeons were more likely to be pressed into involuntary service than ordinary seamen. Threats were sometimes employed to persuade a person whose talents were needed by the pirates. Stede Bonnet once told one prisoner that if he refused to sign, "he would make him the Governor of the first Island he came to; for he would put me ashore and leave me there." A married man was seldom pressed into service against his will. Although a forced man was given the same shares and most of the privileges as a regular member of the crew, he was not allowed a vote. He was watched closely and forbidden to write anyone. If it was discovered that he had, the letter, or any other writing, was nailed to the mast for all to examine. Free Negroes in the crew of a prize ship were given an opportunity to sign the articles, but just as often they would be taken to the West Indies and there sold into slavery. A pressed man who deserted and was recaptured suffered death. Timid volunteers sometimes requested that they be given certificates indicating that they had been forced which they could display at their trials while begging for clemency.

Pirates never enjoyed fighting so much as has been suggested, and they never undertook to engage a prize in battle if it could be avoided. Their object was plunder, not bloodshed. Life for a pirate was easier—and longer—if he could persuade his intended victim to surrender without a fight. If forced into action these dissolute men fought with desperate courage. Yet their courage quite often came from a bottle, for it was customary, on both naval and pirate vessels, to "spirit up" a crew with generous issues of rum. And there were ways of maintaining fervor; for instance, in the crew of Captain Charles Harris was one John Bright who beat "upon his Drum on the Round-House during an Engagement." Many sets of articles provided an extra share for the first man to board a prize.

The popular conception of a pirate ship coming alongside its victim and throwing out grappling irons to bind them together was not considered the best way to engage. One of the more successful tactics was a planned collision, with the pirate vessel slipping across the bow of an intended prize whose bowsprit would become entangled in the rigging of the pirate. This denied the victim the use of his artillery, while the pirates were delivering point-blank enfilading fire. Meanwhile, boarders used the bowsprit as a bridge to clamber across onto the deck of the prize. Equally effective was the firing of chain shot, or "Two-headed Angels," through the rigging to destroy maneuverability. Pirates were reluctant to fire their heavy cannon into the hull of an intended prize lest it sink before they had a chance to plunder its cargo.

They were more willing to grant quarter if no resistance was offered—a policy they publicized at every opportunity. If a captain proved obstreperous and persisted in fighting, he was sometimes shot without ceremony once the ship was taken, another fact that they did not fail to make known. Usually, pirates refrained from plundering the personal belongings of the officers and crew and, depending on storage space in the hold, took only selected items from the cargo. If a cargo proved uninteresting, it was then that the officers and men of a prize were plundered of their personal gear. It was not unknown for pirates to take a liking to the captain of a prize and to bestow presents on him before allowing him to go his way. In 1699, pirates took two sloops off the Carolina coast, one loaded with logwood from Central America, the other with a cargo of rum. They took the rum aboard their own vessel, but apparently liking the captain, gave him the logwood from the other prize. This relatively mild treatment of victims gave captains and crews little incentive to risk their lives for the sake of a cargo.

Prisoners, on the whole, were treated fairly decently. If a prize could be used in the pirate business, the prisoners were either given the pirates' old ship or placed ashore where they could be easily rescued. If the captured ship was allowed to continue on its voyage after it had been looted, often the masts would be cut off short to prevent the crew from reaching port too early and spreading the alarm. The only prisoner who might suffer corporal punishment was the captain, who was sometimes flogged by the pirates if his crew reported that he had been an overly cruel disciplinarian.

Not until there was a determined and concentrated drive against pirates and a number of their profession were hanged did they begin to exhibit that cruelty toward their prisoners so often attributed to them. It was almost as if they had declared open warfare on honest folk. One of the milder treatments during this latter period was delineated by one captain: "They used us extremely hard, beat us, pinched us of victuals, shut us down in the night to take our lodgings in a water-cask, detained us until they had careened their ship and fitted her out for sailing and then . . . gave us our liberty." Another favorite torture was placing matches between the fingers, toes, and behind the ears of the prisoners, usually to make them tell where valuables were concealed aboard ship.

Women prisoners, according to the usual set of pirate articles, were to be treated well. There were practical reasons for this. For one thing, women on a ship could create a great deal of discord. One account states that when a woman was taken among the prisoners, a sentinel was placed over this "so dangerous an instrument of division and discord." Yet the same account goes on to declare that the appointed sentinel "happens generally to be one of the greatest bullies, who, to secure the lady's virtue, will let none lie with her but himself." But this procedure seems to have been more the exception than the rule, for if it became known that women prisoners were customarily treated gently by the pirates, the more likely would a ship with women passengers ask for quarter. This is not to say that women prisoners were never persuaded to share sensual pleasures, or were not forced, for among such scabrous individuals as pirates moral niceties were better spoken than practised. As one buccaneer so succinctly put it, "Some of us engaged in friendships with our women prisoners, who were not hard-hearted." This more genteel treatment of the opposite sex did not apply when there were Negro women among the prisoners.

There was one curious custom prevalent among the buccaneers called "*matelotage.*" When two friendly pirates wished to marry the same woman in a port town, they tossed coins to determine which would go through with the ceremony. The other, however, known as a *matelot,* would have his time with the bride. The husband would purposely leave home when the *matelot's* turn fell due, and the friend would be received in the home to enjoy all connubial pleasures without the responsibilities.

The idea of pirates forcing their prisoners to walk the plank appears to have been a fabrication of later generations. They had methods of dealing with undesirables that made walking the plank seem merciful. It has been said that Stede Bonnet was the only pirate captain to force his prisoners to walk the plank, but the rather full account of his trial (in which many things of a far more sinister nature are documented) makes no mention of his disposing of his victims in this fashion. The formality of a plank seems a bit absurd when it was so much easier just to toss a prisoner overboard. The Elizabethan gentleman turned pirate, Thomas Cobham, allegedly once sewed a group of prisoners into sail cloth and had the whole squirming package thrown into the sea.

Pirates exercised greater cruelty in maintaining discipline among themselves than in their treatment of prisoners. One of their constant anxieties was that a member of their company might desert and provide damaging evidence to the authorities. For this reason, every man was required to sign on for the duration of the voyage, and no one was allowed to retire until he had secured the consent of the entire company, even though he might agree to forfeit his share of the booty. If he deserted and was captured, the quartermaster was empowered to have him shot immediately. One deserter from Stede Bonnet's crew was allowed to select the four men who were to form the firing squad, but he had been such a likeable chap that his life was eventually spared.

The punishment of marooning was often meted out to a pirate apostate, one who deserted his assigned station in battle, deserted from the ship, or stole from the company. This word is derived from "maroon," a corruption of "cimaroons," originally applied to escaped Negro slaves who founded a West Indian community, but eventually came to mean lost people. Pirates were sometimes called, and even termed themselves, "marooners," because of their attachment to this practice. The procedure consisted of putting a man on a desert island (and the Caribbean was spotted with countless little sandspits) and leaving him there to die. More than likely this sand strip would be submerged at high tide. Customarily he was given a pistol and a little ammunition with which to kill himself when the tide washed over his refuge, or when hunger and thirst could no longer be endured. A similar punishment was reserved for one who would steal from a shipmate. After his nose and ears were slit he was placed ashore, not necessarily in an uninhabited place, but where he would be certain to meet with hardships aplenty before reaching civilization again.

Life at sea was monotonous, for a pirate crew was too large to employ all seamen in working the ship. Idle hands bred mischief. When a crew punished one of their own kind, it gave little thought to leniency; a certain discipline had to be maintained at all costs. Those who committed more serious offences were brought before a pirate jury to be tried. Often the sentence was keel-hauling, a practice that dated back to the ancient Greeks. A rope was tied under the victim's arms, another around his ankles. He was thrown overboard and hauled beneath the hull from one side to the other. Even if the culprit survived drowning, his body was badly shredded by the barnacles clustered below the water line. If the jury voted death, little time was consumed in executing the verdict as the condemned man was unceremoniously thrown into the sea. If the pirates were bored and needed a spectacle, the tedium was eased by hanging the condemned man from the yardarm.

Perhaps the greatest personal weakness among pirates, both ashore and at sea, was their passion for strong drink. There are instances on record when a pirate crew was too drunk either to attack a prize or defend itself. It was because of this, and the great fear of fire at sea, that many pirate articles declared that all drinking should be done on deck. A lesser by-product was the many quarrels that arose during drinking bouts. It was for this same reason that gambling, with either cards or dice, was prohibited on shipboard.

Crews sometimes broke off from the parent company and struck out on their own. First, however, a prize suitable for the pirate business would have to be taken, and then the consent of the captain and the rest of the crew had to be gained. This was not always easy, especially after the competition for rich prizes grew tense. Should they slip away without this permission, the original company might well run down and execute the deserters.

One of the most persistent and exaggerated myths about pirates is that of buried treasure. True, some did hide their plunder in the ground, but more money has been spent searching for it than has ever been uncovered. In the first place, pirates were such spendthrifts that they seldom accumulated enough treasure to bury. With such an uncertain future, these men were determined to live for the present. A small group of pirates were known to have spent as much as two or three thousand pieces of eight in a single night, distributed among gambling halls, taverns, and brothels.

A carefree attitude toward life was not confined to piracy; it was a characteristic of the eighteenth century. Death came on with a terrifying suddenness—in the midst of battle, by shipwreck, in a tavern brawl, or as a result of scurvy or some exotic tropical disease. Then, too, there was always the hangman's noose awaiting every captured pirate. On occasion, pirates were not allowed the formality of a trial, being hanged with little ceremony from the most convenient yardarm. But, in general, pirates were taken ashore to have their day in court.

The trials of pirates were traditionally held in admiralty courts, tribunes which had been in existence in England since 1340 for the trial of all crimes committed beyond the high water mark. Several of the less resolute members of a pirate crew often would turn King's evidence and testify against their former shipmates, but they did not receive pardon until after the others had been convicted. Once convicted, a pirate had little time in which to prepare himself for his flight into eternity, for he could be hanged any time ten days after his sentencing.

The hanging of pirates, as were all hangings, was considered a spectacle

The gibbet and the hangman's rope awaited any man who went a-pirating.

Three pirates hanging by their wrists at Gallows Point, Port Royal, Jamaica.

and drew large crowds. The condemned were supposed to have been taken to the place of execution in a procession, led by a functionary who carried a silver oar over his shoulder, the symbol of admiralty authority. The silver oar was used in Massachusetts, but there is no record to suggest that it was so utilized in other colonies. The place of execution was in a public place near the water. A witness in England in 1551 reported that "the punishment for corsairs is to hang them in such a way that their toes well nigh touch the water; so they are generally hanged on the banks of rivers and on the sea-shore." The condemned men were usually made much of by the local clergy; especially ministers like Cotton Mather of Massachusetts, who viewed a hanging as an excellent opportunity to spread the Word. Pirates were used as prime examples of human degeneracy, and Mather seized upon their demise to preach his famous "hanging sermons," laced with lengthy prayers and powerful verbiage.

Pirates were urged to announce their conversion to the paths of the righteous in their last speech just before they were swung off the cart beneath the gallows. Rev. Mather particularly encouraged such protestations of faith and, it is to be suspected, put words into the mouths of the sinners—for he often published these confessions along with a sermon that he particularly relished. Consider, for instance, this extract of a condemned pirate's words placed in such a context, and encased in such syntax as most pirates would have been humiliated to use:

I greatly bewail my profanations of the Lord's Day, and my disobedience to my parents, my cursing and swearing, and my blaspheming the name of the glorious God, Unto which I have added the sins of unchastity. And I have provoked the Holy One at length to leave me unto the crimes of piracy and robbery, wherein I have brought myself under the guilt of murder also. But one wickedness that has led me as much as any has been brutish drunkenness. By strong drink I have been heated and hardened into crimes that are now more bitter than death to me.

Just before they were executed, some pirates seemed repentant, some frightened, some surly, while others told crude jokes, bowing facetiously to the crowd, or went to their Maker with a defiant snarl on their lips. One pirate, hanged in the West Indies, kicked off his shoes as the noose was adjusted about his neck, at the same time declaring, "some Friends of his had often said he should die in his Shoes, but he would make them Lyars." One quaint custom was that each condemned pirate was often given a nosegay of flowers to clasp in his manacled hands as he stepped into space.

Little respect was paid to the mortal remains of a pirate. Ordinary and lesser-known members of the fraternity were buried face down "within flux and reflux of the Sea," below the high water mark where the ceaseless ebb and flow of the tide soon obliterated all evidence of their existence. Bodies of the more notorious captains were embalmed in tar, encased in an iron framework or chains, and then hung from a gibbet at some prominent point along the water's edge, there to sway in the wind until nothing was left of the body, a gruesome example to those who might yield to the temptations held out by piracy.

III

THE BIRTH OF A GOLDEN
AGE

*"dreams of mountains of gold, and happy
robberies."*

Along the coast of North America, the two areas most favored by pirates were the waters off Charleston, in South Carolina, and off
Virginia's Chesapeake capes. Charleston they preferred because the
massive bar that blocked the mouth of the harbor allowed heavily laden
ships to sail forth only at high tide. The capes were popular because most
of the shipping of Virginia and Maryland was funneled through the
narrow mouth of the Chesapeake Bay, between Cape Charles and Cape
Henry, into the Atlantic. And Charleston and the Chesapeake were the
two most important and wealthiest port communities in the southern
colonies.

Piracy came early to Virginia, almost with the founding of the colony.
In fact, one fear expressed by the Spanish government was that the
establishment of Virginia would provide a primary base from which
Spanish shipping would be preyed upon.

The first recorded instance of piracy in Virginia occurred around 1610.
This came about when thirty "unhallowed creatures" were sent in the
pinnace, *Swallow,* to trade with the Indians for food to alleviate the
desperate situation at Jamestown. They were partially successful in their
trading efforts, though not without some violence. Then, with a supply of

food aboard, they decided to go a-pirating. The "most seditious of them" conspired together, forced others to join them, and seduced the remainder "with dreams of mountains of gold, and happy robberies." Their amateurish efforts met with little success; after aimless wanderings at sea, some joined with other pirate crews while others resolved to return to England, swearing an oath "to discredit the land to deplore the fame, and to protest that this their running away, proceeded from a desperate necessity." Yet this was not to be unique to Virginia, for in nearly all colonization ventures men of weak resolve were weaned away from the hardships of the land by the promise of wealth to be gained on the sea.

Throughout the seventeenth century there were scattered incidents of piracy in Virginia. In 1660, for instance, when England was at war with the Dutch, Governor William Berkeley complained that the "Seas are soe full of Pyrates that it is almost impossible for any Ships to goe home in safety." And by 1678, Algerine pirates plundered so many ships off the Virginia coast that the local merchants and planters began to demand convoy service for ships that carried their goods.

As the seventeenth century eased into its last quarter, pirates had come to be something of a necessary evil in many American colonies. They were accepted, for not only did they bring in specie and pay their score like good fellows, but they brought in plunder that could be bought cheap and sold dear. "If the pirates have not supplies and a market for the goods that they plunder and rob," wrote Judge Robert Quary, "they would never continue in these parts of the world." Some colonial governors protested the practice, but it is to be suspected that they were among those who did not receive a share of the pirate gold.

Virginia shared little in this surge of prosperity. There were no heavy concentrations of population to provide a market for pirate goods, nor were there urban delights on which to squander money.

Consequently, Virginia was an object of plunder rather than an outlet for the disposition of pirate booty. Most of the local forts were dilapidated, some destroyed during Bacon's Rebellion, others allowed to fall into ruins through neglect. And in any event, forts were not much defense against pirates, who could operate in the broad bays and estuaries outside the range of land-based artillery. The rural nature of the colony almost invited pirates to come ashore, raid plantations along the coast, and slip away before the alarm could be given. In 1682 one such crew forced their way into and carried considerable property away from the homes of Rebecca Leake and John Williams on Tindall's Point. The Council of Virginia authorized William Cole to fit out a small armed vessel to clear the area of such pestilences. It likewise forbade anyone to serve as a pilot for ships suspected of being pirates.

Cole's little ship, manned by eighteen officers and men, was unable to capture any pirates, and in fact could do little to prevent pirates from coming into the Chesapeake whenever they pleased. Cole's most important function was to give a timely warning if he spotted a pirate vessel. Many of those who did come in were English privateers, sailing under English commissions, who nevertheless held few qualms about attacking an English merchantman should the opportunity present itself. The situation worsened to such an extent that Charles II forbade English men-of-war "to come so near our Coasts as to give an occasion of fear to our merchant ships," while privateers operating under foreign commissions were not allowed to bring their prizes into either English or colonial ports.

Five of the Tindall's Point marauders were taken by Rhode Island authorities and sent back to Virginia in irons, along with a goodly portion of their loot. First imprisoned in Middlesex County, they promptly escaped. The two who were recaptured, one a native of Poland, were tried in Jamestown, convicted, and sentenced to be hanged. The night before their scheduled execution, they once again broke away. Although their escape was successful, their subsequent behavior was bizarre. Three days after their flight, they broke into the same jail via the same window through which they had escaped and then sent word to the sheriff that they were back in prison. Now, they declared, they were ready to die, as they had escaped only to secure enough time to prepare themselves to meet their Maker. So unusual was this behavior that several petitions were sent to the governor soliciting a conditional pardon for such worthy men. Governor Culpeper was so impressed that he reprieved the men until the King's pleasure was known.

When Lord Culpeper arrived as governor, in 1682, the question of pirate depredations had become critical in Virginia. The governor's instructions included a charge to employ every available inhabitant in

"withstanding all Enemies, Pyrates and Rebels both at Land and Sea.
. . ." The Council of Virginia, alarmed by the flourishing piracy off their
coast, recommended that a portion of the Crown revenue be appropriated
to maintain a garrison of sixty soldiers and an armed ketch to protect the
Chesapeake area.

The temporary expedient of sending an armed ketch out into the bay
did little to deter piratical activities. One Roger Jones, who had come out
to Virginia with Culpeper, was placed in command of the vessel and as a
result of his office acquired what was later to be termed "a great Estate."
Although Jones commanded a crew of only eight men, he constantly drew
pay for twelve. But his greatest gains came as a result of "his advissing,
trading with & sheltering severall Pyrates & unlawfull Traders, instead of
doeing his duty in Seizing them." And, it was charged, rather than do
anything that might antagonize the pirate John Cook, Jones had actually
struck the King's colors to him. As soon as the sea rovers discovered that
Jones was of the "tribe or a well-wisher to them," they released his boat,
bestowing a quantity of French wines and other valuable goods on him as
presents.

Then there were the smalltime operators, or occasional pirates, apparently persons of some standing in their neighborhood, who would gather
in the darkness and row out to plunder small coasting vessels that lay
anchored for the night. All of this action, plus the obvious inefficiency of
Jones's operations, increased the clamor for a sizeable ship of His Majesty's navy to be stationed in the Chesapeake as a guard ship. Originally,
it had required an impending war with the Dutch for compliance with
such requests. The frigate H.M.S. *Elizabeth* had been dispatched to
Virginia, but had been burned by the Dutch in one of their incursions in
1667.

When Francis Howard, Baron Howard of Effingham, arrived to assume the duties of governor of Virginia in 1684, it appeared that matters
might improve. Almost immediately he issued a proclamation, warning
all those who might be tempted to indulge a tendency to "Entertain,
harbour, Conceale, Trade, or hold any Correspondency, in any kind, with
any Privateers or Pyrates, upon any pretence whatsoever . . ." lest they be
"prosecuted as Notorious Offenders, and shall be lyable unto such paines,
punishments, and poenalties, as by Law shall be Judged against them."

This was not too effective against the large companies, but Effingham was able to report in 1685 that "some Pilfering Pyrates have done damage to the Inhabitants, but I have taken the Chieftest and executed them."

To pirates, proclamations were but so many pieces of paper fluttering in the wind. Homes along the shore were still plundered, despite the presence of the armed ketch, H.M.S. *Quaker,* and two local sloops, all under the command of Captain Thomas Allen. Now a pattern was beginning to reveal itself. One Roger McKeel would come a-pirating in Chesapeake Bay and then quickly scurry back out through the capes and into the shallow sounds and rivers of North Carolina. That colony, just to the south of Virginia, was already becoming known as a pirate haven. Official letters of protest to the governor received but scant notice. Seth Sothel, not only governor but a proprietor of the colony, held a certain affinity for pirates; but in this Sothel was not unique.

During this period H.M.S. *Deptford,* under Captain John Crofts, was also stationed in Virginia to aid the *Quaker,* but proved just as ineffective. "My footmen," complained Effingham, "would make as good captains as they." Crofts proved too fond of the bottle and, it was said, beat his officers until they were "black and blue all over." His wife, of a most volatile temperament, sometimes created such scenes aboard as would have made an engagement with pirates welcome. Perhaps the best clue to the ineffectiveness of the guard ships is a contemporary description of Crofts: "Belching out a thousand oaths," he declared he had "come into the country to get an estate, and that he would get one before he left." In securing his future, the captain was not above seizing items that he fancied from the cargoes of peaceful merchant ships. All censure was answered with a storm of abuse heaped upon the critic. Fortunately for the trade of Virginia, Crofts and eight of his men were drowned when a sudden squall capsized the *Deptford.*

So many colonies were welcoming pirates that a royal proclamation in 1684 warned against harboring such felons. Governors were urged to enforce this edict. At the same time, it was suggested that the various colonies pass an act similar to the one recently passed in Jamaica, which stated that all those who openly consorted with pirates should be treated as confederates. All piracy trials, once such an act was passed, could be conducted in vice-admiralty courts under royal commissions as authorized

PLATE 1.

SNOW

BRIG

BILANDER

KETCH

Four of the larger types of sailing vessels common to the seas in the eighteenth century.

Smaller sailing vessels used for coastal trade primarily in European waters, although records show the capture of such vessels by pirates in the Atlantic Ocean off the Virginia capes.

under a parliamentary statute of the reign of Henry VIII. Under the Jamaica Act, militia officers were allowed to press as many men as they felt necessary to take a pirate operating in the immediate vicinity, and all persons who resisted such authority could be slain on the spot. Yet, in only a few colonies was there such an act passed, and even then it was in imperfect form and poorly executed.

In 1687, Sir Robert Holmes had been sent out with a squadron to the West Indies to suppress piracy. Temporarily, his authority superseded that of colonial governors. He was but a step above failure in the islands, and the fact that his authority had been delegated to deputies on the mainland further complicated all local action. In Virginia, his representative was Captain Thomas Berry.

In the fall of 1688, a legal controversy flared in Virginia when Captain Simon Rowe of the frigate H.M.S. *Dunbarton* seized three alleged pirates: Edward Davis, Lionel Wafer, and John Hinson. These men claimed they had come from Bermuda to Pennsylvania and from there to Maryland, where they had surrendered to Captain Allen of H.M.S. *Quaker* under the terms of the King's proclamation of August 6, 1688, offering clemency to all reformed pirates. In support of their story they presented certificates signed by Maryland justices of the peace. In that colony they had purchased a small shallop to sail across the bay to Virginia, where, they declared, they planned to settle down as respectable citizens along Chesapeake Bay. At the mouth of the river they had been stopped and searched by Captain Rowe, who placed them under arrest, at the same time seizing a quantity of money, plate, linens, and silks on the grounds that they had been taken in piratical activities.

Some rather damaging information was supplied by Peter Cloise, a Negro who had been taken up with them and whom Davis claimed as his property. In claiming the benefits of the King's proclamation, the men were allowed to make a confession. Not until they had signed this confession did the governor inform them that they had not surrendered themselves but had been taken by a representative of the government, and thereby were not eligible for the pardon promised in the proclamation. Effingham held them in jail at Jamestown until the pleasure of the Crown was known. There was little else he could do. The Crown, unhappy with the mild treatment accorded pirates in the colonies, had directed that no

pirates were to be tried in America unless so ordered by Sir Robert
Holmes. Too often in the past pirates had been hastily, or even illegally,
tried and acquitted before all evidence could be assembled against them.

There was not much doubt that these men had been pirates. In fact,
Davis has been termed "undoubtedly the greatest and most prudent
commander who ever led the forces of the buccaneers at sea." Davis and
Wafer had first visited Virginia in the crew of Captain John Cook in
April, 1683, coming in from the West Indies with two prize ships, one a
French merchantman with a cargo of fine wines. One of the prizes, armed
with eighteen guns, they renamed the *Revenge* and spent some time
refitting her as a pirate ship. Apparently they were able to make the
changes at their leisure, with Roger Jones, captain of the local guard ship,
offering them protection in exchange for a quantity of wine. Not until
August 23, 1683, did they sail out of the Chesapeake on a cruise that
eventually ended as a plundering expedition in the Pacific. In this crew,
Davis served as quartermaster.

A Dutch prize of thirty-six guns, a "lovely shipp," taken off the Guinea
coast, was converted to their use, and renamed the *Batchelor's Delight*.
Soon afterwards, Cook died and Davis was named captain in his stead.
Lionel Wafer, a man of education with some medical experience, was
named surgeon. Davis became one of the most successful of all pirates, at
one time commanding a fleet of ten ships and over a thousand men. So
much loot was gathered in plundering Spanish ships and towns in the
Pacific that it was estimated that each man received 5,000 pieces of eight
in one share-out. They had just returned to the West Indies in 1688 when
word of the King's proclamation arrived. Davis, Wafer, and Hinson
decided to retire from piracy. After selling the *Batchelor's Delight* to a
syndicate of South Carolinians for use in expeditions to the Red Sea,
Davis, Wafer, and Hinson took passage to the continental colonies.
Captain Edward Davis had commanded an expedition that had lasted for
over four years, yet during the entire period his authority never seems to
have been questioned. He had likewise gained a reputation for being able
to restrain his men from extreme acts of cruelty.

Perhaps the one thing that swayed opinion against the three prisoners
was that their possessions were so valuable. They had brought with them
several chests, weighing from four to five hundred pounds, filled with

broken silver plate, gold coins of all nations, and silver melted down into bullets, valued at between £5,000 and £6,000. Too many saw an opportunity for personal gain. To the pirates' petition that their possessions be restored, the answer was that only Sir Robert Holmes or his deputy, Captain Berry, held the authority to determine if they were eligible for the King's pardon or if they should be returned to England for trial. Captain Berry, at the time commanding H.M.S. *Deptford,* eventually came into port and declared that according to his instructions he could not proceed to trial unless the pirate loot was placed in his care. With that the Council ruled that since the men had stated that they were coming in voluntarily, that if they gave security for their good behavior, they might journey to England to seek the King's pardon.

Almost immediately a dispute arose between Berry and the Council as to who should retain custody of the impounded treasure. Everyone wanted to share in the booty, including Captain Rowe who had kept some valuables belonging to the accused men and had refused to turn them over to anyone. Berry demanded that everything be handed over to him. The Council, applying some twisted reasoning, refused this demand on the grounds that the men had not been actually seized, but were coming in to surrender voluntarily of their own accord. They eventually ruled that the entire amount be sent to England. Still the ex-pirates had to post a bond of £500, and it was also ordered that £300 and ten pounds of plate be placed in the custody of Ralph Wormley to be used for payment of all debts that might arise out of the case. Each of the alleged pirates was given £30 of his own money to pay his expenses on the voyage to London.

On March 10, 1692, four years after they had been taken by Rowe, Davis, Wafer, and Hinson appeared before His Majesty's Privy Council in London. Although in the opinion of Governor Effingham and Captain Berry the men were guilty and should be hanged, the Privy Council ordered them released and pardoned. This attempt by these three men to reform and settle down to enjoy the fruits of their adventures had been a costly experience. Many hands had reached into the coffers. It has been suggested that in exchange for their freedom they had agreed to a deal, apparently engineered by Dr. James Blair, who was in England at the time promoting the idea of a college in Virginia. Davis, Wafer, and

Hinson agreed to donate £300 and one fourth of the valuables still held by Captain Rowe to the new college. Later, the College of William and Mary rather discreetly referred to this gift as "By money obtained of the Privateers."

Despite the efforts of Captain Rowe, guard ships offered limited protection on the Virginia station. In 1691 it was discovered that the *Dumbarton* was unserviceable; she was beached, broken up, and her guns transferred to the fort on Tindall's Point. H.M.S. *Wolf* and H.M.S. *Henry Prize* had been assigned briefly to the Chesapeake, but proved to be greater nuisances than of any real help. Captain Purvis of the *Wolf* was a poor sailor and ran his ship aground. Captain Finch of the *Henry Prize* was so timid that every time an alien sail was sighted he retired to the protection of the guns on Tindall's Point, declaring the strange vessel was too formidable for him to attack.

Most of the guard ships before 1691 had been sloops or ketches, but in that year there had arrived from Ireland H.M.S. *Dover Prize,* a frigate.

H.M.S. *Apollo,* a frigate comparable to those stationed in Virginia waters to protect the merchantmen plying back and forth between England and her wealthy colony.

Her captain was Thomas Pound, a former pirate. Pound was familiar with Virginia waters, although originally he was from Falmouth (present day Portsmouth), Maine, and had cruised primarily off the New England coast. Two years earlier, in September, 1689, in the midst of the debate about Davis, Wafer, and Hinson, Pound's ship, the *Mary* had been blown into the Chesapeake during a hurricane. They put into the York River and remained there for eight days, unmolested because the *Dumbarton* had been careened at the time. When finally captured, Pound had been saved from the gallows in Boston through the influence of a "Mr. Epaphus Shrimpton and Sundry Women of Quality." Forswearing his piratical ways, Pound was given a commission in the Royal Navy and shortly afterward placed in command of the *Dover Prize*. He arrived in Virginia April 17, 1691.

The presence of Pound seems to have frightened pirates away from the Chesapeake area for the time being. Yet piracy flourished outside the capes amid constantly changing interpretations as to who should be adjudged a pirate, a situation brought about by the changing diplomatic alignments in Europe.

One such case was that of Captain William Whiting who came into Virginia in October, 1695, and was promptly accused of piracy. He had taken a Spanish ship at sea, an incident that normally would have been overlooked, but at this time England was allied with Spain against Louis XIV of France. Despite the war, had Whiting carried his prize into a West Indian port, one suspects that little attention would have been paid him. Virginia, under Governor Edmund Andros, seems to have been following instructions from England more than some other colonies, and Whiting found himself in the custody of the sheriff and his ship impounded. He was ordered back to England for trial by the admiralty court. Aboard his prize were a number of Indians who were to have been sold as slaves by the Spanish, but were now "declared free Indians and accordingly to have their liberties."

Virginia received a vigorous opponent of piracy when Francis Nicholson returned as governor in 1698. Nicholson had earlier expressed himself on pirates with "I confess that I have always abhorred such sort of profligate men and their barbarous actions; for sure they are the disgrace of mankind in general, and of the noble, valiant, generous English in

particular, who have the happiness of being governed by so great a King."
As governor of Maryland he had berated Governor William Markham of
Pennsylvania for the latter's alleged affinity for pirates. On one occasion
he had sent an armed body of men into Pennsylvania in pursuit of a
pirate by the name of John Day and his "gang of brisk fellows," and the
incident erupted into a jurisdictional dispute with Governor Markham.

In those colonies where there was surplus cash, piracy became a lucrative field for investment. Many wealthy persons formed syndicates to fit
out pirate vessels, sharing the plunder with the crews. At first, these ships
were sent out to prey on Spanish shipping in the West Indies, but toward
the end of the seventeenth century they discovered a more profitable and
less hazardous area in which to operate, the Red Sea, where the shipping
of the "infidel" Moslems could be plundered. This was but an illustration
of the basic premise that pirates were attracted to concentrations of wealth
when those who held that wealth did not have the strength to defend it.
So lucrative was this Red Sea freebootery that many young men of good
families signed on as ordinary seamen in the crews of such infamous
characters as Thomas Tew. Yet this was not magnet enough to draw the
attention of all pirates away from the North American coast. They
continued to operate out of the Bahamas, "still . . . a common retreat for
pyrates and illegal Traders."

Few colonial governors were not tarred by the brush of piracy. William
Markham of Pennsylvania was one of the worst offenders. Markham,
lieutenant governor from 1694 until the arrival of William Penn in 1699,
was titular head of the Quaker, or Proprietary, faction in Philadelphia. A
pamphleteer was to write in 1703: "These Quaker have a neat way of
getting money by encouraging the pyrates, when they bring in a good
store of gold, so that when [John] Avery's men were here in 1697, the
Quaking justices were for letting them live quietly, or else they were
bailed easily." William Penn reported that in London the gossip was that
the Pennsylvanians "not onlie wink att but Imbrace pirats, Shipps and
men." Markham gained a reputation as a "Steddy freind" of pirates and,
it was charged, sold protection for £100 per man. He had allowed his
daughter to marry one James Brown, a pirate of some note who had
sailed with John Avery. Not only did this couple associate with the
leading families of Philadelphia, but Brown was able to gain a seat in the

Assembly, although that body, in 1699, expelled him as being "unfit to sit here." Other ex-pirates apparently found it easy to don the cloak of respectability in Pennsylvania. Captain Robert Snead became a justice of the peace with little more trouble than the payment of money to the proper persons. Yet when Snead attempted to prosecute pirates, Markham issued warrants against him. And to facilitate the entire relationship, Markham applied for the position of collector of customs in addition to his executive duties.

The leader of the opposition, or Anglican faction, Judge Robert Quary, charged that Markham openly associated with pirates and entertained them at his table. And Quary was a person who should have known a pirate when he saw one. Colonel Quary had been secretary of South Carolina and, at one time, acting governor. But after he had allowed pirates to openly land their goods in the Ashley River the Lords Proprietors had removed him from office. In 1689 he had been appointed chief justice of the Court of Common Pleas, but lost that post when he was once again suspected of trafficking with pirates. It wasn't until 1697 that he was restored to favor with an appointment as judge of the vice-admiralty court of Pennsylvania, and there pursued pirates with as much vigor as he had defended them in the past. In this he was supported by William Penn, who feared that open association with pirates would lead to the revocation of his charter.

New Jersey played the pirate game too, assisting them in such ways as scheming to provide safe harbors for them. There was no fort to fend off pirates had the authorities so desired, and some professed to believe that because the Jerseys were not immediately under the authority of the King, pirates could not be seized or punished in that colony. "Not a magistrate of this country," complained Robert Quary in 1699, "will concern himself, but exclaims against me for disturbing the men that bring money into the country."

Not too far away, near Lewes, Delaware, there was a more secluded pirate retreat in the estuary known as the "Hore Kills." This spot was attractive to the sea rovers because it was poorly defended and also afforded easy access to both Philadelphia and New York. Lewes had been twice devastated in pirate raids, in 1672 and 1699, but these had been foreign pirates and, in reality, little more than privateers. In general,

Delaware was receptive to pirate visits. When one naval officer became too vigorous in his pursuit of pirates, the people of Newcastle threatened to arrest him and throw him into prison. The colony became a favorite careening and victualing area, but after Pound came to Virginia, the pirates were somewhat chary for fear that he would sail up from the Chesapeake.

Boston was noted for its courtesies to pirates. In 1690, it was reported that condemned pirates were allowed their freedom if they were able to pay "£13 6s. 8d. or be sold into Virginia" as indentured servants. Six years earlier when a French privateer, or pirate, arrived off Massachusetts, Boston merchants dispatched a pilot to guide him safely into port, where he was unmolested as he sold his plunder and refitted for sea. It was reported that this crew shared out at £700 per man, leaving the greater part of it behind, "having bought up most of the choice goods in Boston." It was common knowledge that a number of pirates regularly refitted for sea at one of the numerous small ports in the colony. Edward Randolph reported that the noted Red Sea pirate, Captain Thomas Tew, came and went as he pleased, with the merchants of Boston as his best customers. The governors of Massachusetts, it was whispered, grew rich from bribes, with Sir William Phips actually inviting pirates to come from Philadelphia to Boston, "assuring them their liberty to trade."

In New England, however, Rhode Island was considered "the Chiefe Refuge for Pyrates," and became something of a clearing house for merchandise brought in by the freebooters. One account stated that at Newport there was a "greater plenty of European goods than in any place in the Main, tho' they have not so much as a vessel that goes there from England." One charge was that because the colony was governed by "either Quakers or Ana Baptists," it had grown to be "a free port to illegal traders and pyrates from all places." In April, 1694, when Thomas Tew came in with loot of gold and silver valued at £100,000 plus a "parcell of Elephants Teeth," the ivory was quickly purchased by the merchants of Boston. Such success invited emulation and many vessels were fitted out in Rhode Island for the Red Sea venture.

Connecticut governors, it was said, did not molest pirates because the governors were elected annually and they wished to do nothing that might antagonize the powerful merchant groups. And Connecticut, as other New England communities, was a trading colony and desperately needed the coin brought in by the pirates to maintain a reasonable balance of trade with England.

Other colonies were equally guilty. New York witnessed regular visits from the Red Sea pirates, while the east end of Long Island was a favorite hideout and victualling spot for the pirates. Their presence was tolerated after it was pointed out that traffic with the pirates brought an estimated £100,000 a year into New York.

Governor Benjamin Fletcher, his secretary, the collector of customs, and even the captain of the New York guard ship, H.M.S. *Richmond,* were all supposed to be in league with the pirates. It was common knowledge that protection could be purchased from Fletcher if the price was right, usually £100 per man, and privateering commissions could be obtained for around £300. The pirates also gave him "presents," including one prize ship which he sold for £800. The governor, as did Markham of Pennsylvania, openly consorted with and entertained notorious pirates, some at his dinner table. Thomas Tew was observed riding in Fletcher's coach through the streets of New York in friendly conversation with the governor. When questioned about such intimacy, Fletcher's pious excuse was that he wished to reclaim Tew from the vile habit of swearing. If taken up, legal proceedings against such people as Tew were quietly dropped, while the guard ship never seemed quite ready to put out to sea when pirates were reported off the coast. In June, 1695, a charge against Fletcher stated that, "We have a great parcel of pirates, called the Red Sea men, in these parts, who get a great booty of Arabian gold. The Governor encourages them, since they make due acknowledgements." So flagrant were Fletcher's operations that his successor recommended that he be taken up and sent to England for trial.

Among southern colonies, the two Carolinas were the two prime pirate sanctuaries. South Carolina was known as a place where the freebooters were welcomed, and some of its governors had grown wealthy dealing with them. Governor Seth Sothel, former governor of Albemarle (North Carolina) who had once been captured and held for ransom by Algerine pirates, had sold commissions as privateers for twenty guineas each, and openly carried on trade with pirates. And, before the people of Albemarle banished him, it was charged that he had seized the property of respectable merchants, claiming they were pirates, one of whom "dyed of grief and ill usage." Governor Philip Ludwell had dealings with one James Miller, a pirate of Scotch origin who later went to Philadelphia, where he was protected by Markham. When John Archdale was governor in 1693, seventy pirates came in from Jamaica to Charleston with a "vaste quantity of Gold from the Red Sea, they were entertained, and had liberty to stay or goe to any other place. The Vessell was seized by the Governor for the proprietors as a Wreck & sold, they have no regard for the Acts of Trade." The Council did go so far as to expel one of its members, Lieutenant John Bone, from membership. Others who were censured for their associations with pirates seemed to lose little in prestige, even when thrown into jail. In answer to repeated protests, an occasional pirate was executed to placate critics. But even then only a certain class were taken up for punishment, as explained in the observation: "there were abt half a dousin Pyrats lately hang'd in Carolina, but it was because they were poor. . . . These rich ones appear'd publickly [in Charleston] and were not molested in the least." When the proprietors, fearful of losing their charter, made strong efforts to control the situation, it resulted in the rise of a strong anti-proprietary faction. Not until the pirates began to take the ships carrying cargoes of South Carolina rice was there any great change in the attitude of the people.

North Carolina, however, was the one area that promised continued annoyance for Virginia. More and more it became apparent that "Carolina is too ordinary a Receptacle of Pyrats." Because of little trade and the lack of suitable harbors, North Carolinians became eager purchasers of pirate goods. The shallow sounds along the coast provided safe asylum as well as locations for careening and provisioning pirate ships. North Carolina became, according to Edward Randolph, surveyor-general of customs in America and ardent foe of piracy, a "place which receives Pirates, Runaways and Illegal Traders." Herndon Walker, president of the Council and acting governor, Randolph declared to be "in no sort fit for Office." When H.M.S. Swift ran aground in North Carolina, these "barbarous people" seized and burned papers connecting them with piracy. In general, it had become apparent that proprietary colonies carried on more illegal trading, and harbored more pirates than the royal colonies. Proprietary governors were never so efficient as they should have been in the suppression of these filibusters.

Edward Randolph declared that no pirates were sheltered in Virginia. Francis Nicholson, he noted, was a man "truly zealous to suppress Pyracy & illegal Trade." Yet there were some ex-pirates in the colony. In 1696, at least sixteen of the crew of John Avery, the famous "Arch-Pirate" who had been so successful off Madagascar, were sentenced to be transported to Virginia as indentured servants.

The most notorious case arising out of the Red Sea hysteria was that of Captain William Kidd. His story deserves to be repeated, for his name has become synonymous with piracy, and his voyage, at the time and ever since, has been a point of controversy. Actually, Kidd was little more than a pale facsimile of some of the other pirates of his day.

William Kidd was the victim of a reform movement. A respectable citizen and property owner of New York, he had gained some renown as a privateer and at one time had operated something similar to a packet line between New York and London. In 1695 he happened to be in London when the powerful East India Company was demanding relief from the increased activity of pirates in the Near East, which had forced the company to sail its own vessels in convoy. Ships of the Royal Navy, being engaged in the war against France, could not be spared for operations against the Red Sea men.

Because of the continuing and increasing outcries against Benjamin Fletcher, Richard Coote, the Earl of Bellomont, was preparing to sail for America to assume his duties as governor of New York and New England, areas considered to be "infected with those two dangerous Diseases," evasion of the Navigation Acts and the harboring of pirates. Colonel Robert Livingston, member of the Council of New York, was also in London at this time and went to Bellomont with the word that Kidd had agreed to undertake a voyage against the Red Sea pirates. The captain was recommended as "a bold and honest Man, and he believed fitter than any other to be Employ'd on that occasion."

William III accepted this proposal, reserving for the Crown a tenth part of all plunder taken on the expedition. Although Bellomont's name was the only one appearing on the Articles of Agreement, other promoters included the Lord High Chancellor, the First Lord of the Admiralty, and two Secretaries of State who contributed £6,000 to the venture. Kidd and Livingston put in an additional £1,500.

The *Adventure Galley,* a new ship mounting thirty-four guns was fitted out. A crew was carefully selected. But before the ship cleared the Thames, a large portion of Kidd's crew had been pressed for service aboard the men-of-war of the Royal Navy. This meant that Kidd now had to replace them with what riffraff he could persuade to sign on. The captain's commission empowered him not only to attack and bring in enemy ships as prizes, but specifically instructed him to destroy or bring in such noted pirates as Thomas Tew, John Ireland, Thomas Wake, and William Mace.

On the voyage to New York a French prize was captured. Before sailing from New York, Kidd had to fill out his crew and found it again necessary to recruit "men of desperate fortunes and necessities" to the number of 155. He sailed for the Red Sea. His adventures thereafter become somewhat clouded, but one contemporary account suggests that Kidd was not so much a victim of circumstances as has been claimed, and that out-and-out piracy was in the back of his mind from the beginning. One Edward Barlow, captain of the *Septer,* an East Indiaman, reported that Kidd had successfully attacked several Moorish vessels. He also had heard at Calcutta that Kidd had come into that port for wood and water and had boasted "that he was sent out by the King of England and had his comishon to tack pirates or French. But hee turned pirat him self."

According to the evidence presented at his trial, Kidd took and plundered a number of French, Moorish, and Portuguese ships. On January 30, 1698, he had captured an Armenian ship, the *Quedagh Merchant,* richly laden with a cargo worth £4,500. Sailing under the French flag, it would seem to have been a legal prize for an English privateer. Shortly afterwards, at Madagascar, many of Kidd's crew left him after a share-out was made—with Kidd taking some forty shares for himself. The *Adventure Galley* was leaking so badly that Kidd went aboard the *Quedagh Merchant.* Subsequent events suggest that the *Quedagh Merchant* was in the employ of the East India Company and sailing under false colors, for that organization complained bitterly that taking the ship was a simple case of piracy. Their influence was such that the Lord Justices of England issued orders that Kidd be apprehended.

Although Kidd presented no direct threat to Virginia, the cry raised against him and the captain's subsequent return to America led to apprehensions within the colony. Governor Nicholson alerted all militia commanders and sheriffs to arrest Kidd should he appear within their jurisdictions. The situation assumed a critical air when Kidd put in to Delaware Bay briefly before continuing his voyage to Boston. This took on an added significance when the sheriff of Accomac County reported that Kidd was operating off the Virginia coast and he apparently planned to continue in the area, for he had sent for his wife, although she refused to join him. The new guard ship in Virginia, H.M.S. *Essex Prize,* sailed to the Delaware in an effort "to look After about Sixty Pyrates (wch belonged to one Kidd) who came in from Madagascar." There was no sign of them.

For awhile it appeared that Virginia might become a refuge for pirates who had sailed with Kidd. The sixty men who had deserted Kidd in Madagascar and had come into the Delaware Bay region to share their loot, were reported to be coming into Virginia to settle down. Nicholson didn't want them. Judge Quary of Pennsylvania attempted to arrest some of them, but received no cooperation from Governor Markham. In fact, certain Pennsylvanians openly supplied the pirates in return for the opportunity to purchase their loot. Nicholson was warned that eight or nine of the group had boarded the sloop of a "Rogue" by the name of Gravenrod and were sailing for Virginia, there to lose themselves among the population. Others of Kidd's men who had escaped from prison were also reported bound for the colony. If the rumors could be believed, there was a veritable influx of ex-pirates streaming toward Virginia, although few were ever reported as arriving.

It was during this period of alarums that Kidd sailed into Boston and was suddenly arrested by Bellomont. There being no law providing for the trial of pirates in the colonies in 1699, Kidd was taken to England in chains. His case had become an issue between the two contending political parties of England. Even then, the captain was tried not only for piracy but for the murder of William Moore, the gunner on the *Adventure*

Galley, whom Kidd had termed a "Saucy Fellow and a Lousie Dog." Moore had been killed, or so the evidence stated, when Kidd, during a fit of passion, struck him in the head with a water bucket.

The political ramifications had become the most important issue by the time Kidd arrived in England. He was called before the House of Commons in an attempt to fix guilt upon those who had sent him on the expedition. The captain didn't do much to aid his cause. He was half-drunk when he appeared before the examining committee, and behaved in such a contemptuous fashion that one of the members was led to exclaim: "This fellow, I thought had been only a knave, but unfortunately he happens to be a fool likewise."

During his trial, William Kidd constantly asked to be allowed to examine the papers that had been taken from him. He claimed that amongst them were French passes taken from the *Quedagh Merchant* and another ship which would have made them legitimate prizes. He declared that he was unable to prepare his case without them, or to contradict the "Multitude of downright Lies [that] were whispered to prepare Mens Minds." The passes had indeed been among the papers that Bellomont sent to England, and had been printed in the Journal of the House of Commons, although Kidd seemed unaware of this. And, it was charged, the trial had been rushed into court before all the papers had arrived. Over 200 years later, the originals were discovered among manuscripts in the Public Records Office. The papers, it seems, had been deliberately suppressed.

Despite Kidd's declaration that "I am the innocentest Person of them all, only I have been sworn against by prejudiced Persons," he was convicted for the murder of William Moore and on three counts of piracy. On May 23, 1701 William Kidd was hanged at Execution Dock. He didn't die easily. The first time he was swung off the rope broke, and he spoke to the crowd while the rope was being adjusted for the second time, "professing his charity to all the world, and his hopes of salvation through the merits of his Redeemer." So ended the saga of Captain Kidd, a pirate by circumstance and political machinations, either a villain or a martyr, but one who caused more commotion in the colonies than many a more vicious man, and who became known in Virginia as "That Great Rogue Kidd."

Perhaps too much attention was paid to the Kidd affair and not enough energy expended in clearing the coast of more dangerous pirates. Certainly their numbers had multiplied, perhaps because of this concentration of effort on a single felon. In 1699 and 1700 American waters had become infested with freebooters of all nationalities. So many captured pirates were "escaping" from jails that William III issued a proclamation demanding that jailers guilty of allowing such prisoners to escape be punished "with the utmost severity of the Law. . . ." All captured pirates in the future were to be sent to England for trial with the least possible delay.

By the turn of the century, many of the northern ports that had formerly demonstrated some tenderness towards pirates, now began to harass them, although it was by no means an unanimous effort. In part, the change of attitude was due to the Earl of Bellomont, governor of New York, and partially because the pirates were becoming careless as to whose ships they took. Still, there was little hope that piracy could be abolished in these waters. Bellomont was convinced that the only way to suppress piracy was for the home government to send over honest governors, judges and attorneys-general, and to increase the number of guard ships. When, however, Bellomont became too active in his campaign against pirates, a number of merchants dispatched petitions to London requesting that he be recalled and Fletcher returned to New York as governor.

Despite Nicholson's vigorous efforts to clear Virginia waters of the pirate clan, more prizes were being taken in the Chesapeake. A possible explanation is that Thomas Pound had been recalled and his *Dover Prize* had been replaced by the *Essex Prize*, Captain John Aldred commanding. Aldred was a timid sailor and a bit on the querulous side. His presence practically invited pirates to come in.

Because admiralty courts in the colonies had no power to try pirates except under a local law, much time was consumed in arguing about the passage of a statute for punishing pirates and privateers. Little was accomplished. Even the King's promise that "all such Pirates as shall be forwardest to surrender themselves and most ingenious in their Confession shall have the surest grounds to hope for his Royal Mercy," influenced few to change their way of life. The beginnings of the eighteenth century promised a period of crisis for all the North American colonies.

IV

THE FRENCH PIRATE AND THE BOLD GOVERNOR

"certainly we are in a State of War with the Pirates."

During the summer of 1699, matters reached a critical stage along the coasts of Maryland, Virginia, and the two Carolinas. There were too many pirates operating off the Atlantic shore to provide booty for all. No longer were they on the prowl for only the more glamorous plunder of jewels and precious metals; they seized every cargo for which there was a market, even such commonplace products as tobacco. Not only were prizes deprived of their lading, but they were forced to give up guns, ammunition, provisions, rigging, sails, and even some of their crew members. Many vessels, stripped of their gear, were left floating as helpless as a bit of flotsam.

The pirates were growing bolder. Shortly after daylight on July 26, 1699, the *Maryland Merchant,* out of Bristol bound for Virginia, spied a sail in Lynnhaven Bay, an inlet at the mouth of the Chesapeake. At almost the same time the stranger was spotted by Captain Aldred of the *Essex Prize.* Bearing down on him, Aldred ran up the royal colors; the other ship ran up her "bloody Flag." The pirate opened fire as both ships maneuvered for position. The pirate, either attempting to board the naval vessel or force her into the shallow waters near the shore, pulled in close. A brief but brisk defense by Aldred kept her at a distance.

Spreading all sail, the *Maryland Merchant* attempted to flee into the James River. The pirate broke off his engagement with the *Essex Prize* and bore down on the merchantman. When he failed to gain the wind, Aldred fell away for fear the pirate would board him and overpower his short-handed crew, inasmuch as seven of his men had been ashore filling the water casks when the pirate was sighted. At length, the pirate ship came up with the *Maryland Merchant,* hailed her and bade her heave to lest she be boarded with no promise of quarter. Richard Burgess, captain of the merchantman, immediately dropped anchor and went aboard the other ship, a "clean tailored" vessel of twenty-six guns and 130 men.

The ship, which the crew alternately referred to as the *Providence Galley* and the *Alexander,* had but recently been taken from William Rhett of South Carolina, and was one of a pirate fleet that had been cruising outside the capes. Their captain was John James, an ugly, squint-eyed, pockmarked Welshman, who delighted in terrifying his prisoners by declaring that he was Captain Kidd. Burgess was told, as he stepped on board, that "they would not hurt the haire of any man's head, and would not damnifie the Ship but would deliver her to me again." When Burgess, in answer to a flood of questions, declared that he did not know the actual strength of the *Essex Prize,* the captain laughed and replied that he already knew. A few days earlier he had taken from a packet boat the books and accounts that Aldred was sending to the Admiralty in England. This had been, he continued, one of the reasons that they had been so bold as to venture within the capes.

Satisfied that the naval vessel was no stronger than represented in the papers, the pirates set out in pursuit of the *Essex Prize.* Aldred bore away before the wind, firing his stern guns. The pirate followed, occasionally sending forth a shot from her bow chasers, her captain bellowing that he would give good quarter and that they only wanted to supply themselves with the necessary naval stores. The *Essex Prize,* firing as rapidly as possible (one witness said that she fired over 200 shot), bore for the shore, hoping to force the *Providence Galley* into unfamiliar waters. James, guessing Aldred's intentions, fell away and sailed back to the *Maryland Merchant.*

The pirates were more in need of provisions than loot, for the plate of a Mr. Pops, a passenger, valued at £100 failed to interest them. They did take the mainsail, the topsail, nine pipes of water, 100 casks of bread, the rigging, a new hawser cable, and about £100 worth of dry goods. They also prevailed on seven members of the crew to sign the pirate articles. The *Maryland Merchant,* when finally released, was so disabled that she could make no headway and ran aground in the Elizabeth River.

It was near seven o'clock the following morning when the sloop *Roanoke Merchant* sailed into Lynnhaven Bay. This ship, belonging to Judge Robert Quary of Philadelphia and captained by Thomas Jones, was bound for Annapolis from Barbados. They spotted the *Providence Galley,* but made no attempt to steer off, for the pirate was flying the royal colors. When within range, the pirates fired two guns, a signal for Jones to come aboard their ship. He did. He was fascinated by the crew, each of whom wore a gold chain around his neck, while a gold toothpick dangled at the end of the one worn by the captain.

Captain James demanded the pork, peas, and tallow listed in the cargo of the sloop. Then he had his fun by loudly swearing that he would burn the *Roanoke Merchant,* apparently just for the pleasure of hearing Jones beg. After stripping the sloop of the items they wanted, the pirate crew voted to go to sea again. Seven men of Jones's crew were forced, against their wills, to join the pirate crew. Jones continued his entreaties not to burn his vessel until James tired of the fun and allowed him to continue his voyage to Annapolis. The *Providence Galley* stood out to sea through the capes.

That the pirates had sailed so cooly within the capes and had demonstrated so little fear of the *Essex Prize,* led to much consternation and apprehension. Lookouts were posted at strategic points along the shore, while the militia of the counties bordering the bay were alerted to hold themselves in readiness for immediate service. Although the pirates did not again soon venture into the Chesapeake, they did come in on the Eastern Shore where they "killed & wounded several Beefs."

Pirates lurked off the Virginia shore until late in the fall. In November, the *John Hopewell* of London was plundered by a pirate who called himself Henry King, and who persuaded nine members of the *Hopewell's* crew to sign articles. Although the rough seas of winter drove the pirates to seek protected harbors and a warmer climate, they returned in even greater numbers in the spring of 1700. Their success encouraged others to take up the trade. For instance, when it became known that pirate crews were seeking additional seamen, some aboard merchantmen mutinied and joined the first pirate ship that came along.

Matters were not helped by the growing antagonism between Captain Aldred and Governor Nicholson. They were both testy men, easy to anger and wearing their vexations on their shoulders as a mantle. One irritation for Aldred was the extraordinary number of desertions from the *Essex Prize,* so much so that the captain sent an almost constant stream of requests to the governor that he be allowed to press local inhabitants to bring his crew up to its authorized complement of sixty seamen. Some of his men had jumped ship with as much as twenty months pay owing them. When granted press warrants by Nicholson, Aldred used them with little discretion, forcing into service such valuable artisans as carpenters when there were already more then enough in his crew. On one occasion he seized a prospective bridegroom on the eve of his wedding. Some whispered that Aldred was little better than a pirate himself, for he would hold a ship, accusing its captain of piracy until a specified bribe was paid.

Relations worsened between the governor and the captain. Aldred refused to cooperate with Lieutenant Colonel William Willison, commandant on the Eastern Shore, when the militia were called out in anticipation of a possible pirate incursion. When Nicholson sent Peter Heyman, collector of customs, aboard the *Essex Prize* to check the size of the crew, Aldred refused to allow him to make the count. In September, 1699, Nicholson himself had gone aboard the naval vessel, demanding to speak with the captain. Aldred, pleading illness, remained in his cabin with what he termed the "Country distemper." The governor immediately placed the captain under arrest, confining him to his cabin under guard. When released from arrest a week later, Aldred termed the governor's actions as "silly, impertinent, and full of pride and vain glory."

If one must take sides, Nicholson should be favored, for he was doing everything within his power to protect the Chesapeake area without antagonizing the people. In fact, Aldred admitted before the governor and Council that the weak and defenseless condition of the *Essex Prize* was partially his responsibility. And it was the governor who had the vessel brought up to Archer's Creek and properly victualed. Simmering animosity continued beneath a surface of genteel cordiality. Aldred constantly submitted excuses for not setting out on a cruise against the pirates, complaining of the possible danger from storms and rough seas. When there were reports of a small ship, suspected of being a pirate, anchored at Smith's Island, Aldred assured Nicholson of his zeal for action, but there was no one aboard his command familiar with those waters, and he grumbled of his "false friends, and malicious Vexations & Accusations." Had pirates chosen this period to come into Chesapeake Bay, they could have sailed in with impunity.

Things looked brighter in early 1700. The *Essex Prize* was recalled to England, to be replaced by a thirty-gun, fifth-rate ship, H.M.S. *Shoreham,* commanded by Captain William Passenger. The new guard ship arrived in April, "the most dangerous time for them [pirates] coming upon this coast." Several vessels were convoyed out through the Capes, but before the month was out there was to be livelier action.

Sunday, April 28, 1700, began as just another balmy spring day. Governor Nicholson was at Kecoughtan, sealing up dispatches and letters to be sent to England. The *Shoreham* was anchored offshore, filling her water casks. The *Essex Prize* lay careened, getting her bottom scraped preparatory to her return voyage to England. Captain Passenger had come ashore and, along with Governor Nicholson, was enjoying the hospitality of a Colonel Wilson. The gathering was interrupted by Aldred who came ashore with the information that he had just been aboard a pink that had but recently escaped from a pirate in Lynnhaven Bay.

Everyone sprang into action. The governor issued orders calling out the local militia and dispatched warnings to all ships in the river. Nicholson demanded that Passenger wait until he had finished, but the captain excused himself and was rowed out to his command. His watering party was recalled and all ships in the vicinity were requested to send men to reinforce the crew of the *Shoreham*. Eight seamen were sent from the *Essex Prize*. As quickly as possible, Passenger weighed anchor and steered for Lynnhaven Bay, but he was slowed by contrary winds and night fell too quickly. The pilot refused to venture into shallow waters in the darkness and, about three leagues (ten to twelve miles) from the alleged pirate, the *Shoreham* dropped her hook. Meanwhile, Nicholson had checked the readiness of the militia on the south shore, although one unfriendly to the governor suggested that the delay came about because of "some weighty pretences." About ten that night Nicholson, accompanied by Captain Aldred and Peter Heyman, came aboard the *Shoreham.*

The pirate ship anchored in Lynnhaven Bay bore the unlikely name of *La Paix,* and was commanded by one Lewis Guittar. The crew, near 150 men, were all French with the exception of two Dutchmen and one Englishman. The dimensions of this well-built ship of Dutch construction were eighty-four by twenty-five feet. Her flush decks mounted twenty iron cannon. She had originally been in the Dutch Surinam trade, but after her capture and conversion by the pirates (who set her captain adrift in a small boat), she had experienced success in the West Indies as a pirate vessel. The *La Paix* was the flagship of a pirate fleet of four vessels, all under Guittar's command.

There had been good hunting off the capes for the *La Paix* and the pink and two sloops accompanying her. They had arrived in the area around April 20, when they took the pink *Baltimore,* John Lovejoy, master. Two days later they captured the sloop *George* of Pennsylvania, Joseph Forrest, master. As soon as the cargo was plundered and the crew taken off, a fire was started in the sloop's cabin, while the carpenter of the pirates bored a hole in her side. The *George* lay burning and sinking as the *La Paix* and her consorts steered for Cape Henry.

On April 23, about thirty leagues off Cape Henry, they came up with the *Barbados Merchant* of Liverpool, bound for Virginia, William Fletcher, master. The pirate pink, which had no heavy armament, bore down on the *Barbados Merchant,* came alongside, and her crew of sixty men soon overwhelmed Fletcher and his men. At first they showed kindness to the captives, but the congenial atmosphere quickly changed

A pink was a small, maneuverable sailing vessel often favored by pirates.

when they received no favorable responses to the invitation to sign their articles. Blaming Fletcher for the reluctance of his men, they stripped the captain and beat him with the flat of their cutlasses, and would have killed him had not one of the pirates interceded in his behalf. After forcing the carpenter and one seamen to sign the articles, the pirates aboard the *Barbados Merchant* cut away the masts, sails, and bowsprit, hurling them all overboard. They took away all candles, smashed the compass, and sliced away a large portion of the rudder to leave the prize drifting helplessly and perhaps to bring a slow death for the crew who had been so foolish as to reject the jolly life of a pirate. Unbeknownst to the pirates, the foremast, its sails, and rigging lay tangled over the side. After the pirate pink sailed off, Fletcher and his men fitted up a jury rig and slowly made headway toward the capes.

The following day the *Pennsylvania Merchant,* Samuel Harrison, master, bound from England to Philadelphia, lay becalmed about twenty leagues off Cape Henry. As the breeze swung up, the *La Paix* and one of her attendant sloops came into view. The *La Paix* ran up the Dutch ensign to allay suspicion. As the pirates swung around to gain the weather gauge, she sent her "bloody Colours" aloft. As Guittar attempted to gain the wind, Harrison maneuvered out of danger. Shortly afterwards he hailed the *Barbados Merchant,* at this time still attempting to rig her jury mast. Before Harrison could offer assistance to the wallowing wreck, the *La Paix* came up, bidding the *Pennsylvania Merchant* strike her flag. Once again Harrison steered off and managed to evade the pirates through the night. As the pirates drew within range the following morning and opened fire, Harrison struck his colors. The crew were treated roughly and, because the cargo held few items of interest to them, the pirates stripped and robbed the thirty-one passengers and seamen of the captured ship. Harrison was informed that he was a lucky man, for when a Dutch ship had offered resistance, a number of the crew had been hanged at the yardarm. There was talk of burning the *Pennsylvania Merchant,* as the crew felt that Harrison should be punished for his evasive tactics. Two days after her capture, the *Pennsylvania Merchant* was left blazing in the open sea.

The primary purpose of the *La Paix*'s master in coming into the Chesapeake was to rerig the ship and fill the water casks. On April 28, the

Indian King, Edward Whitaker, master, was outward bound for London. She was a Virginia-built ship and was described as "one of the most beautiful merchantmen." Her colors were lowered just as soon as she was hailed by the *La Paix.* The crew and passengers were "violently and with force of Arms" taken aboard the pirate ship with their arms bound behind them. Amid the terrifying threats and gestures, their pockets were rifled as the *Indian King* was conducted back toward Lynnhaven Bay.

That same day, and shortly after the capture of the *Indian King,* another vessel was taken. The small *Friendship* of Belfast, Hans Hammel, master, was outward bound for Liverpool with a cargo of Virginia tobacco. The pirates bore in, delivering a volley of small arms fire, killing Hammel. As the *Friendship* hove to, four pirates came across to the prize. One of them, John Hoogling by name, and pilot for the *La Paix,* at first pretended to show some sympathy for Hammel, but suddenly cried out that it had been he who had killed the master. He was roaring with laughter as the prisoners were herded into the forecastle. The *Friendship* was brought back into Lynnhaven Bay.

As they drew into the bay, they sighted the *Nicholson,* whose master, Robert Lurtin, had just given orders to weigh anchor and begin his voyage to London. The *La Paix* slid up, wearing no colors. Lurtin hailed the stranger, but his only reply was a shout of "Out of the Sea, you Dogs," followed by a volley of small arms fire. Lurtin slipped his cable, hoisted sail, and attempted to flee. He managed to outmaneuver the heavier pirate ship for near two hours until his main yard and topsail were shot away. The *Nicholson* was a clean sloop and caught the fancy of the pirates who planned to convert her to their own use. Sails and provisions were removed from the *Indian King* to the *Nicholson.* With the exception of one man, the prisoners were forced to labor at this task. The carpenter aboard the *Nicholson* had stated that there was a guard ship in the Chesapeake; the majority of the other prisoners had declared that there was none. Because the carpenter had obviously lied, the pirates removed the flint from a musket lock and slowly screwed the metal into the flesh of his thumb. When they tired of this amusement they began to beat him, crying out "that he should not lye the next time." Meanwhile, the hold of the *Nicholson* was cleared, its contents thrown overboard, and the waters of the bay were soon littered with floating tobacco. Over 100 hogsheads of tobacco were heaved over the side, along with clothing and several bolts of cloth that did not strike the fancy of the pirates. This operation was still going forward when the *Shoreham* came up on the morning of April 29, 1700.

At three o'clock that morning the *Shoreham* had weighed anchor. An hour later the dim outlines of the *La Paix* could be sorted out from among the shadows of the grey dawn. Captain Passenger had. steered within a mile of the pirate when the topsails of the *La Paix* began to flutter loose. Guittar's plan was to get to the windward of the naval vessel and then pull in close enough to board. Passenger guessed the strategy and kept the weather gauge, firing a shot across the bow of the *La Paix*. Guittar ran up his "Blood red Colours." The engagement was joined around five in the morning, with both ships loosing broadsides when within range of each other.

The pirates held nothing but contempt for the *Shoreham,* referring to her in shouts as a "Dogg," a "Toad," and "Damn her, she is but a little thing and we'll have her presently." They bolstered their courage by boasting that they were strong enough to repel any ship afloat. To the prisoners, Captain Guittar did not seem to be as much a leader in battle as he should have been. John Hoogling, "a man in great Esteem" of his shipmates, appeared to be the real leader. Some forty or fifty prisoners were locked into the hold once the firing began. Other captives had been working aboard the *Nicholson*. Their guards, discovering beer on board the sloop, had drunk themselves into a near stupor by the time the *Shoreham* opened fire. Whether angered by the appearance of the naval vessel, or at being awakened, the guards took out their irritation upon the prisoners by beating them across the backs with leaded rope ends.

Much of the battle was conducted within pistol-shot range; the *Shoreham,* sailing better than the *La Paix,* managed to stay to windward. Governor Nicholson, Peter Heyman beside him, stood on the quarterdeck during the entire engagement, both firing small arms across at the enemy. Nicholson excited the courage of the crew by promising them "plenty of gold." Captain Aldred behaved with "great courage." Shortly after noon, Heyman plunged to the deck, killed by a shot from the *La Paix*.

The *La Paix* slowly disintegrated under the continuous pounding. By four in the afternoon her masts, yards and rigging had been battered "all to shatters," several guns were dismounted, and Passenger was confident that he had beat them "to pieces." Guittar, in attempting to draw out of range, put his helm over. As the ship came slowly about, she suddenly ceased to respond; the rudder had been shot away, there were no sheets or bowlines to haul the sails and the thick hail of lead had driven the pirates from the deck. The *La Paix,* her sails slack and drifting aimlessly, shuddered to a stop as she ran aground. Passenger dropped anchor in three fathoms of water and waited.

The *Shoreham* rocked gently amid the sudden quiet as the red flag on the *La Paix* fluttered down. Although too badly beaten to continue the fight, Guittar was determined to gain the best possible terms. A powder train had been laid to thirty barrels of gunpowder and he now threatened not only to blow up his own command, but the prisoners as well. The terrified captives began to plead that some effort be made to inform the governor of their plight. With that, one of the prisoners, Baldwin Mathews, leaped overboard; the others felt that he was going to swim over to the *Shoreham,* but Mathews decided to save his own skin and struck out for the shore. As he did, the pirate company began to chant "broil, broil," leaving the prisoners to understand that they would all burn together unless quarter was granted. One John Lumpany, with the permission of Guittar, swam over to the *Shoreham* to inform Nicholson that there were English prisoners aboard the pirate ship and to repeat the terms under which Guittar would surrender.

Between four and five o'clock that afternoon, Nicholson wrote out the terms he was willing to grant to Captain Guittar of the "Laypaste." Quarter would be granted to all pirates who would surrender themselves, but they would be sent to England for trial and Guittar and his men would be referred "to the Mercy of my Royal Master King William the Third. . . ." Guittar accepted. The battle was over.

Passenger lost four men killed during the engagement, one of whom was Peter Heyman. There could be no accurate accounting of pirate casualties. At least twenty-five or twenty-six had been killed, and there were twelve or fourteen wounded, eight of whom were destined to die within the next two weeks. During the fight the pirates had thrown many of their dead over the side, and there were suggestions that many of their badly wounded had been gotten out of the way in the same manner. In all, about 120 prisoners were taken. Carried ashore, they were placed under the guard of the militia of Elizabeth City County.

In June, 1700, 111 captured pirates were sent to England in irons, dispersed in twenty-eight ships, a precaution felt necessary to prevent a concentration of prisoners from overpowering the crew of a single vessel. Lewis Guittar was almost alone in the *George* of Plymouth. The convoy was under the protection of Captain Aldred in the *Essex Prize*. So great was the fear that there would be a rescue attempt that the *Shoreham* furnished additional protection for forty or fifty leagues out to sea, "that being reckoned the distance within which pirates cruize." Nicholson was aboard the *Shoreham*.

Three pirate prisoners did not make the voyage. James Hoogling, Cornelius Franc, and François Delaunce had leaped overboard before Guittar surrendered. They had been captured on shore. Hoogling had escaped, but was retaken shortly afterwards. Since they had not been taken at sea, it was felt that they were not entitled to the terms of the surrender and therefore fell under the jurisdiction of the Virginia General Court. Their trial was held in May before the other prisoners had been returned to England. Those destined for trial in England were examined and depositions taken from them. Their story, including that told by Guittar, was that they were not real pirates, but had been forced to join the company against their wills. Hoogling, Franc, and Delaunce all swore that they had deserted the *La Paix* to save their lives when they feared that the remaining members of their crew were going to blow up the vessel. According to the testimony given by their shipmates, all three had shown fear when it appeared that the fight was going against them. Cornelius Franc, when brought out on deck after the battle, had cried out, "Must I be hanged that can speak all Languages?" His chief defense was that he had been pressed by the pirates solely for his linguistic abilities. Another of the pirates also declared that he had been forced, and in battle he had always pointed his cannon up into the air or down into the water, although constantly cursed by his shipmates for his poor marksmanship.

Once it was established that these three were guilty of piracy, they didn't have a chance. The attorney-general forecast their doom as he declared piracy to be "the worst of all crimes and Pyrates the worst of Men, Nay by their base Actions they degrade themselves below the rank

of Men and become Beasts of prey and are worse than the worst of
Enemys for they are governed by no laws of Nature or of Man's, they
never give quarter nor show mercy but as they please themselves. . . ."
All three were found guilty and the court directed that they be hanged in
Princess Anne County as near as possible to the spot where the *Shoreham*
engaged the pirate ship. Good strong ropes were to be used and their
bodies were not to be cut down, but were to be left hanging until the
ropes rotted and allowed their remains to fall to the ground.

Although these three were to be hanged almost immediately after their
conviction, they were destined to plague Virginia a little longer. While
awaiting execution they broke jail. Nicholson immediately placed a £20
reward on their heads. After their recapture in Accomack County they
were promptly hanged as directed by the court, even before their comrades had been returned to England.

Unfortunately, the capture of the *La Paix* did not bring to an end the
threat of pirates to Virginia. Less than a month after the engagement,
Nicholson pointed out that during the battle Passenger did not have
enough men to work the sails and man the guns at the same time, and
urged that the complement of the *Shoreham* be brought up to its authorized strength. Adequate protection of the area was necessary, "or certainly
we are in a State of War with the Pirates, expecting them upon our
Coasts, and may be within the Capes all this Summer. Those great
Rogues and Enemys to all mankind, are Sensible of their Condition if
they be taken, which naturally makes them very desperate &c." The
governor also urged the establishment of vice-admiralty courts in the
colonies to save time and expense in shipping pirates back to England for
trial. Then, having made his recommendations for improvement, there
was little more he was empowered to do other than issue a proclamation
prohibiting strange seamen from wandering about Virginia.

The pirate pink in Guittar's fleet continued to operate outside the capes.
Although carrying no heavy armament, she captured several merchantmen by her superiority in fighting seamen. One of her prizes was the
Lion of Bristol which, after masts and bowsprit had been cut away, was
left drifting helplessly. This was ironic, for the *Lion* had slipped out of
port without paying customs duties, and it was rumored that her master
himself planned to go a-pirating. One vessel, but recently loaded with

cargo in the York River, the pirates scuttled after they had plundered her. Because they already had too many prisoners, they cast some of the crew adrift in a small boat to make their way as best they could to shore. Both Aldred and Passenger were sent out to eliminate this menace to local shipping, but the pirates had sailed away.

In London, Lewis Guittar and twenty-three of the crew of the *La Paix* were tried, condemned, and on November 23, 1700, were hanged, twenty being buried in "Limehouse Breach." At a later date, some forty additional pirates met a similar fate. The *La Paix* was condemned and ordered sold by the admiralty court, the proceeds divided "according to the Rules and Orders of the Sea." There had been a sizeable debt involved in the affair, to the amount of £420 sterling. This included calling out the militia to guard the prisoners, the making of manacles in which they were ironed for the voyage to England, and the expenses involved in the transportation. Although the House of Burgesses agreed to assume £420 sterling of the debt, to be paid out of an imposition on liquors, it did appear to be an unfair burden. The Council and the House, loaded with the costs of constructing the new capitol in Williamsburg, requested that the remaining costs of capturing the pirates be appropriated from quitrent collections.

Although there were those who swore that Governor Nicholson was little more than a spectator during the fight with the *La Paix*, he immortalized himself by paying for the tombstone above Peter Heyman's grave, the epitaph reading, "In the engagement he stood next to the Governor upon the Quarter deck and was here honorably interred by his order."

So much confusion in the past had resulted from the capture of pirates in American waters and piracy had so increased that it was obvious that legal procedures must be simplified. Until the year 1536 all trials for piracy fell under the jurisdiction of the admiralty courts; but under its rules of procedure, only those who had confessed or were convicted by the testimony of a witness who actually had seen the crime committed could be condemned to death. This had occasioned so many circumventions of justice that a statute passed during the reign of Henry VIII provided that piracy trials should be conducted before specifically named commissioners in certain counties in England, the procedure to be based on common law.

Although this proved more efficient than past statutes, it meant that all those accused of piracy on the high seas, along with all evidence, had to be sent to England for trial, an expensive and time-consuming operation. Because of the tediousness of this process, there had been a general ignoring of the law, or the holding of what might be termed illegal trials for piracy in the colonies.

When the situation began to border on chaos, Parliament, late in 1699, passed an act authorizing certain persons to constitute a vice-admiralty court in the colonies. The governor, lieutenant governor, a member of the Council, and the commander of a ship of the Royal Navy must always be included along with members appointed by the Crown under the Great Seal of England. The weakest part of the statute was the provision that those who were considered accessories to pirates, or who aided or concealed them, were to be sent to England for trial, presumably on the assumption that such persons would be released by colonial courts.

All of this simply meant that it would be much easier to try pirates in the colonies, but first they had to be captured. Despite Passenger's success, prospects for the future did not appear too hopeful. The local guard ship was not strong enough to cope with the situation.

With a crew reduced by illness, Passenger continued to cruise the Chesapeake area. For some time the only piratical activity occurred when some querulous individuals accused their neighbors of piracy and were promptly hauled before the justices for their gossiping. Nicholson, however, had no intentions of being surprised again. A system of lookouts was established along all deep-water coastal areas. And physical aid was on its way. A fourth-rate man-of-war, H.M.S. *Lincoln,* Captain Edward Neville, had been assigned to temporary duty in America and ordered to cruise between Cape Fear and Cape May, although she was to station herself in Lynnhaven Bay "as much as Wind & Weather will permitt." As soon as she could be fitted out, another fourth-rater, H.M.S. *Southampton,* was to relieve the *Shoreham* as permanent guard ship. Until the fall of 1701, both the *Shoreham* and the *Lincoln* were to force all merchant ships to sail under convoy to a safe distance beyond the Capes. The *Lincoln* did not arrive until June, 1701, and with it came Governor Nicholson's commission for trying pirates, authorizing him to take all necessary measures "for the resisting and withstanding all Enemies Pirates and Rebels both at

Centurion (right), a fourth-rate ship of the Royal Navy, engages and captures the Spanish ship *Neustra Senora de Capodongo,* June 20, 1743. The *Centurion* was of the same class as the *Lincoln* and the *Southampton,* guard ships assigned to the Virginia station in 1701.

Land and Sea." Perhaps it was because the proprietary governments of the Carolinas had been too friendly with pirates in the past that Nicholson's commission also allowed "Tryall of Pyrates in Virga. or Carolina or at Sea. . . ." By this time, however, there was little need for additional guard ships or commissions. Queen Anne's War had broken out and the *Southampton* was kept in England, with the *Shoreham* to remain on the Virginia station.

With the advent of war, many pirates now found it easy to gain commissions as privateers and, under this semi-legal protection, cruised in waters that promised greater rewards. Those few instances of reported piracy in Virginia waters seem to have been committed by French privateers rather than actual pirates. Wars customarily brought a technical end to piracy.

V

SUNKEN TREASURE, STRONG DRINK, AND A GENTLEMAN PIRATE

" a Wiff in their bloody Flag"

Few pirates, but many privateers, operated off the Virginia capes between 1702 and 1713, the terminal dates of the Anglo-French conflict known as Queen Anne's War. Apprehensions were just as great as in times of great piratical activity, however, for it was rumored that those sailing under letters of marque and reprisal were none too discriminating in selecting their victims. There were also reports that privateers were plundering other privateers, even though both were sailing under the same flag. To add to the anxieties of the Virginians, there were stories that French men-of-war were actively cooperating with French privateers. So successful were enemy operations that as soon as the new guard ship, H.M.S. *Garland,* arrived, all vessels that sailed in 1707–1708 were compelled to sail out through the capes in convoy.

There was some difficulty from evil persons who operated from land bases. Not pirates in the technical sense of the word, some men in Princess Anne County made a practice of plundering unfortunates who were shipwrecked or were cast away on that shore. Some trouble originated in Maryland, where a sloop, the *Prudent Hannah,* was fitted out and her crew sought their fortunes among the small coasting vessels that plied Chesapeake Bay. Other rumors implied that a number of pirates, sailing

79

Colonel Alexander Spotswood, distinguished soldier and governor of the colony of Virginia, 1710-1722, and implacable foe of the pirates who infested the waters off the Virginia capes.

under the protection of a French commission, had found refuge in North Carolina whence they planned to slip over into the Chesapeake for their plunder.

Tensions were such that many people were willing to believe piracy of almost anyone who was so unfortunate as to be accused, even in jest. One such victim was Thomas Pitton, master of the *Factor*, of Biddeford, Massachusetts (now Maine). Pitton held a British privateering commission and had posted bond in London to insure his proper conduct at sea. In the summer of 1706 he had stopped a small Danish hoy and summoned the captain aboard the *Factor*. A sudden squall made it impossible for the captain and several of his crew to return to their own vessel until the winds subsided. When Pitton was able to make the transfer, he was either given, or took, some wine and molasses for his troubles. When the story reached Captain Low of H.M.S. *Advice*, he immediately accused Pitton of piracy. The Council of Virginia looked into the matter and could find no evidence that Pitton was, or had been, a pirate. After a costly delay, the captain was released and allowed to continue his voyage.

In 1710, a new governor, Colonel Alexander Spotswood, was appointed, a man as zealous as Nicholson in his drive to eliminate piracy. Two years later, a twenty-gun frigate arrived with a royal proclamation calling for a cessation of arms. During the interval before the actual treaty with France, it was, in general, felt that the seas would be safe except for the swarms of pirates that usually infested them after every war. Surprisingly, the Chesapeake was free of pirates, since most of the privateers-turned-freebooters confined themselves to the Caribbean, where the pickings were richer. The Spanish treasure fleets had not sailed during wartime and there was a backlog of rich booty to be had. In fact, the Virginia coast was so free of pirates that Spotswood dismissed a petition by some merchants and planters for an additional man-of-war to patrol the bay. The governor was convinced that the guard ship already on the station furnished sufficient protection and "there's no occasion to put her Majesty to a further Expence untill it appear that ye Pyrats are more formidable than there's yet any reason to apprehend they are."

Alexander Spotswood had failed to understand the lesson of history that piracy mushroomed as an aftermath of every war. The 1708 act that had given the owner and the crew of a privateer the whole of the plunder had, in a sense, established privateering as a profession. In 1713, when the war officially ended with the Treaty of Utrecht, fighting had been going on for a long time. Some seamen had never known anything but life aboard a privateer. Thousands were thrown out of work. Poverty drove them to crime and experience drove them to piracy. There was no great danger involved in the changeover; guard ships were too few and too widely spaced to constitute any real threat. James Logan, secretary of Pennsylvania, estimated that there were no less than 1500 pirates operating off the North American coast in 1717. Despite the publicity given to those few pirates who were captured and hanged on the gallows, thousands of unknown, and perhaps more adept, pirates roamed the seas, unsung but growing rich.

By 1716 the Bahamas, and especially New Providence, were becoming known as a "Nest of Pirates," and a rendezvous for many "loose disorderly People." Spotswood's anxiety was not only for the Virginia coast, but he was the nearest royal governor to those islands and felt some responsibility for them.

Two of the more influential pirate leaders who made New Providence their headquarters were Benjamin Hornigold in the sloop *Mary,* and Henry Jennings in the *Bathsheba.* Under their leadership, the pirates flocking into Nassau were now beginning to refer to themselves as a "flying Gang," and not only took over the town but the entire island of New Providence. Much of their time, or so the reports to Spotswood ran, was spent in "plundering the Inhabitants, burning their Houses and Ravishing their Wives." Many decent folk refused to leave their dwellings for fear of being murdered. By 1716 the situation had grown so desperate that the governor of Antigua wrote, "I do not think it advisable to go from hence except upon an extraordinary occasion, not knowing but that I may be intercepted by the pirates." One by-product of this reign of terror was that Negro slaves became "very impudent and insulting," and there was growing fear of an insurrection. A substantial number of the blacks went off to join those pirates who did not seem too concerned about color differences.

These Caribbean sea rovers put out that they would take only French and Spanish prizes and would not "meddle" with vessels of English registry, but they did not extend this courtesy to colonial ships. And they were not above exacting tribute from those who passed through their

The treasure of the New World was carried in Spanish galleons such as these from Spain's South American colonies, attracting swarms of pirates all along their route through the sheltered waters of the Caribbean to the open sea off the Florida peninsula.

domain, including one Captain Alexander Stockdale who was forced to give them twenty pounds in gold in lieu of a promised flogging. When Captain Thomas Walker grew so brash as to arrest the pirate Daniel Stillwell, Benjamin Hornigold sailed into Nassau harbor, rescued Stillwell, and threated to burn Walker's home down around his ears. Hornigold then made so bold as to proclaim that all pirates in the Bahamas were under his personal protection. Walker fled to South Carolina.

Perhaps the most exciting information received by Governor Spotswood was that of sunken treasure. It was rumored that much gold was being recovered from the wrecks of Spanish galleons that had been sunk off Cape Canaveral on the east coast of Florida during the great hurricane of 1715. In that great wind, ten of eleven vessels of the Spanish plate fleet had gone down, carrying to the bottom a treasure worth at least fourteen million pesos. The lure of "fishing" Spanish wrecks had been strong ever since 1687 when William Phips raised over £300,000 in silver bars and coin from a Spanish wreck near Hispaniola. The prospect of fishing these wrecks appealed to the pirates, and in 1716 Henry Jennings led an armed flotilla of a brigantine and three sloops and had driven off the sixty man guard posted on shore. Within the storehouse they discovered 350,000 pieces of eight that the Spanish had managed to salvage through the use of "diving Engines." They missed the greater treasure, however, for some four million pesos worth of treasure had previously been recovered and moved to Havana.

The Spanish treasure fleet founders off Cape Canaveral in the great hurricane of 1715.

The Spanish later erected batteries to protect the wrecks. The pirates once again drove them off and, after establishing guard ships, successfully fished the wrecks.

Some of this information came from refugees in the Bahamas. Much more was learned from Captain Josiah Forbes, formerly master of the *John and Mary,* whom Spotswood had arrested, along with three others, as pirates in June 1716. Forbes's story was that he and his companions had been cast away on Cape Hatteras before making their way into Virginia. Josiah Forbes was not one to keep his mouth shut. He couldn't restrain himself from boasting of his activities as a pirate and of driving the Spanish away from their shore batteries. It was then that Spotswood had him arrested and thrown into jail. Forbes had promptly escaped, but his stories had been enough to quicken the imagination of the governor.

All this talk of treasure tied in with a growing concern about the increasing number of pirates. The wrecks drew pirates to the mainland, and they might well begin to drift northward. Not only would this endanger the trade with Jamaica, but operations along the Atlantic coast would threaten the important salt works of Virginia. Spotswood was likewise convinced that his commission from William III, entrusting him with the appointment of admiralty courts in the Bahamas, gave him some jurisdiction in the Caribbean. There is also the suggestion, although his reasoning is nowhere delineated, that the treasure recovered from the sunken galleons could constitute a legal British prize and, if so, the governor's share would be one-tenth. H.M.S. *Shoreham,* which had been returned to Virginia as a guard ship, was at this time on a mission to St. Augustine for the colony of South Carolina. In order to check the wrecks, as well as the activities of the pirates in the Bahamas, Spotswood listened more attentively to the proposals of Harry Beverley.

Harry Beverley was a surveyor and a lawyer by profession and was a major of militia, a justice of the peace, and a former clerk of the House of Burgesses. His home was in Middlesex County. Apparently a man of some wealth, Beverley had in the early summer of 1716 launched a sloop, the *Virgin of Virginia,* designed for the West Indian trade.

Hearing of the riches gained from fishing the Florida wrecks, and the report that the Spanish paid well for those ships that aided them in regaining the treasure, Beverley determined to make use of his sloop in this manner. If this plan did not materialize, he considered fishing the wrecks surreptitiously or searching for additional wrecks within waters under British control. If none of these developed, he would sail to the West Indies and there dispose of his cargo of provisions. Beverley applied to the governor to be allowed to crew the *Virgin of Virginia* with forty or fifty armed men, offering to furnish bond as surety for their "Honest & peaceable Deportment."

Spotswood, anxious for additional information of the sea rovers who had taken over the Bahamas, granted Beverley permission to make the voyage as outlined, but with specific warnings not to disturb those Spanish vessels he might meet in the vicinity of the wrecks. England and Spain were at peace, and the governor wished to do nothing that might jeopardize that situation. Recently, the Spanish had been angered by pirates who had slipped in to fish the wrecks and had raised at least 20,000 pieces of eight. Beverley was instructed to render "all necessary assistance in the recovering of what properly belongs to them, contenting yourself with such reasonable salvage for your trouble therein as the Law of Nations is allowed in such cases." Beverley's primary mission, as outlined in his instructions, was to make himself familiar with the situation in the Bahamas. Should he meet the *Shoreham* along the way, Captain Thomas Baker was to assist him in his endeavors. Beverley was cautioned not to endanger the peace between England and Spain by any acts of hostility. If, however, he was attacked by pirates, "you may repel by force, and do your best endeavour to sink, burn & destroy all such pirates or Sea Rovers as you shall meet with. . . ."

Beverley sailed from Virginia June 23, 1716. Two days after he had cleared the capes he was caught up in such a gale that he could make no headway and he found himself near the island of Bermuda when the winds finally died. On the morning of July 5, he was in sight of a Spanish man-of-war, attended by a sloop. Although the *Virgin of Virginia* flew British colors, the Spaniard fired three shots across her bow, ordering Beverley to come aboard. Don Rocher de la Peña, master of the *St. Juan Baptista,* refused to examine Beverley's papers, but demanded to know whence he came. Apparently Beverley had pressed a portion of his crew, for it was these indentured "servants and Indian slaves" who swore that their master was on his way to join the pirates operating out of Jamaica.

With that, a Spanish prize crew was sent aboard the *Virgin of Virginia*. Beverley's men were beaten, stripped of their clothes, and, after the cargo was looted, brought back as prisoners to the *St. Juan Baptista*. With the exception of Beverley and the two mates, the naked Virginians were forced to perform menial tasks aboard the Spanish warship.

By July 30, the *St. Juan Baptista* was in Puerto Rico where most of the goods plundered from Beverley were sold. On August 11, they sailed into the harbor at St. Domingo. In both ports Beverley demanded that the proper authorities be notified and that he and his men be given a proper trial. Not only was this request refused, but he was kept incommunicado and informed that he would receive his just deserts when they reached Vera Cruz. On August 14 Spotswood received a hastily scribbled note that Beverley had managed to smuggle off the ship. After reciting his tale of anguish, he concluded with: "All that I can be certain of gaining by ye voyage, is a Certain Antidote ag'st Popery. We have ridiculous prayers to St. Ignatius and ye rest of their S'ts twice a day, and a General Swearing, lying, Cursing, Stealing, Cheating and all Manner of vice almost all ye rest of ye day & night."

There was no trial at Vera Cruz. Beverley's sloop was sold without legal proceedings. He and his men were denied subsistence of any kind. They were reduced to begging on the streets, while the "assiento factory," the British merchant ship allowed in the harbor under the terms of the Treaty of Utrecht, gave them an occasional handout. Several of his crew starved to death before those still alive were allowed to go to Cuba. Beverley was kept behind as a prisoner in Vera Cruz.

For some time the case of Harry Beverley threatened to become an international incident; but it paled into relative insignificance as Virginia moved into a period of trial insofar as piracy was concerned. The vultures of the sea were beginning to come up out of the Caribbean in increasing numbers. The situation became critical after the *Shoreham* returned from detached duty and received orders to return to England. Using the excuse that the frigate was unfit for sea duty until she had been careened and repaired, Spotswood prevailed on Captain Baker to remain on the Virginia station until his relief arrived. So great had grown the pirate threat that no vessel dared sail out through the capes unless convoyed by a man-of-war. Although her bottom was so fouled that she could not be used in the pursuit of pirates, the presence of the *Shoreham*, it was hoped, would frighten them away from the Chesapeake.

Spotswood also suggested to London that a pardon be granted to those pirates who voluntarily came in and submitted to authority. Every pirate who removed himself voluntarily from the shipping lanes meant that shipping could be considered just that much safer. The situation had worsened by the time that Harry Beverley, after seven months a prisoner, escaped from Vera Cruz and returned to Virginia in August, 1717. His report was that hordes of desperate men were swarming into the Bahamas in expectation of seeking their fortunes on the sea.

This influx of pirates was being felt in Virginia as early as the spring of 1717. By the last of May, Spotswood was complaining that "Our Capes have been for these six Weeks pass'd in a manner blocked up by those Pyrates, and diverse Ships inward bound, taken and plundered by them." One of their chief concerns, reported Spotswood, was to gain new ships to accommodate the burgeoning pirate crews. The *Shoreham,* in her present state of disrepair could only act on the defensive.

One of the most active of the freebooters was Captain Samuel Bellamy, an Englishman whose wife and family still lived near Canterbury. Bellamy, as did several of the more notorious pirates, served his apprenticeship with Benjamin Hornigold. Hornigold, noted for his generosity to prisoners, plundered only French and Spanish ships and refused to yield to his crew's demands that he prey upon those flying English colors. He was deposed by a vote of his crew and sent off in a prize sloop with about twenty-six loyal members of his company. Bellamy was elected captain in his stead.

Bellamy had proved to be a most successful captain in the West Indies, flying "a large black Flag, with Death's Head and Bone a-cross." He fancied himself quite an orator, ofttimes entertaining his prisoners with flowery speeches. Although appearing sympathetic to the plight of his prisoners, he adhered strictly to the wishes of his crew. On one occasion he is reported to have told the captain of a merchant vessel, "Damn my blood, I am sorry they won't let you have your sloop again, for I scorn to do anyone mischief when it is not to my advantage."

By the time that Bellamy arrived off the capes of Virginia in late March, 1717, his ship, the *Whido Galley,* was armed with twenty-eight guns and manned by a crew of near 200 men. The greater part of the seamen were natives of Great Britain and Ireland, with a few other nationalities and colonials listed, including two Indians. There were an unusually large number of Negroes among the crew, about twenty-five, "taken out of a Guinea ship." Working in consort with Bellamy was a blue and yellow sloop, with old patched sails, but armed with twelve guns. About forty pirates made up the crew of this smaller ship and were under the command of a dark-complexioned man who wore a peruke and answered to the name of Paul Williams.

Bellamy ignored outward bound ships with their cargoes of tobacco, preferring the richer cargoes of those coming from Europe. One of their first prizes was the *Agnes* bound for Virginia from Bermuda with a cargo of rum, sugar, and "sundry European goods." She was taken early in the morning of April 7, about five leagues east of Cape Charles. That same day they also captured the *Anne* of Glasgow and a pink, the *Endeavour* of Brighton. Two days later, after plundering the cargo of the *Agnes* and taking the prisoners aboard the *Whido Galley,* they cut away her masts and left her sinking. The following day a ship out of Leith, Scotland, was taken. After removing the articles they wanted from the cargoes, and persuading eight members to sign the articles, they placed most of the prisoners aboard the *Endeavour* and the Leith ship and allowed them to sail away to safety. The *Anne* and her crew they forced to accompany them to assist in careening the *Whido Galley.*

The pirate sloop commanded by Paul Williams was also meeting with some success. As the *Tryal* of Brighton, John Lucas, master, was standing into the capes in the early morning light of April 9, the sloop suddenly darted out from behind a head of land. The *Tryal* offered no resistance. Lucas was held prisoner while his cargo was plundered until late that afternoon, when a strange ship was sighted steering for them. Frightened, the pirates bade Lucas to follow them, but a favorable wind springing up he slipped away inside the Capes.

Bellamy and Williams, when reunited, escorted the *Anne* inside the bay, searching for a suitable careening shore. They bore away when they sighted a ship in Lynnhaven Bay, a ship they feared might be a man-of-war. According to the brags of the crew, who claimed Bellamy and his men had taken no less than fifty prizes, at least fifty companies of pirates would be operating soon off the Virginia coast.

The last prize taken by Bellamy was a Virginia sloop captured off the capes on April 24. The pirates, in careless conversation, were overheard by their prisoners to say that they intended to cruise about ten days off Delaware Bay before spending an equal time off Long Island to intercept ships from Philadelphia and New York to replenish their store of provisions. Then, with seeming boldness, they declared that they were going to careen the *Whido Galley* on Green Island to the east of Cape Sable of present day Nova Scotia.

Matters of small import topple great men, even pirates. Somewhere during their voyage north, Bellamy captured a ship with a large cargo of wine. Seven pirates were placed aboard to oversee its voyage to a friendly port. Stationing one of the prisoners at the helm, the pirates proceeded to sample the cargo; they were soon drunk and continued "pretty free with the Liquor." Their condition was such that they paid little attention to navigating the ship, even after nightfall when a storm blew up.

The prisoner at the wheel, taking advantage of the darkness and the drunken condition of the crew, ran the ship aground in Nossett's Bay near Eastham on Cape Cod. The *Whido Galley,* following the lights of the prize, ground to a stop in the pounding surf. Two prisoners, an Englishman and an Indian were cast up alive on the shore. Lest their remaining prisoners testify against them, the pirates began to murder those still on board; the night was filled with "doleful cries heard on the Shore," and many of the bodies that later washed up bore ugly wounds.

Samuel Bellamy and the eight members of his crew who made it safely to shore were soon captured. Others may have escaped, although it was later stated that 130 of the company were drowned. Brought to trial in Boston, Bellamy and seven of his men were condemned to death on the gallows. One of the crew, Thomas South of Boston, proved to the satisfaction of the court that he had been forced and was acquitted. Before the guilty were executed, the ministers of Boston had a field day, praying with the pirates, preaching to them, examining them, exhorting them, and presenting them with pious books "suitable to their Condition," for "there is not that Place upon the face of the Earth, where more pains are taken for the Spiritual and Eternal Good of the Condemned Prisoners."

In the meantime there had been the royal proclamation promising pardons for all piracies committed before January 5, 1718, if the offenders came in before September 5 of that year. It was specified that they could surrender to any governor or lieutenant governor in the colonies. This was a remarkable document in that the pirates were forgiven all murders they had committed, and they were allowed to retain their accumulated loot. In a sense, it was an open admission that the situation had grown desperate and was out of the control of government.

This document, received in Virginia January 3, 1718, caused no great outcry in that colony, but in the West Indies it was received "with great joy." Some surrendered, but as soon as they knew their past crimes had been wiped from the books, gave in to "the itching desire to return to their former vile course of life." Among the more prominent pirates who came in were Benjamin Hornigold and Henry Jennings, with Hornigold later commissioned by Woodes Rogers to hunt down his former colleagues in the pirate business. Nevertheless, there was no reduction in the numbers of pirates. A substantial number of recruits came in when the Spanish attacked and drove out the English logwood cutters in the Bay of Campeche; it was estimated that nine of every ten pirates during this period were unemployed logwood cutters. By June, 1718, there were near 3,000 pirates operating out of New Providence alone, so many that few merchant ships dared sail without a strong escort. Once again, competition forced many pirates to sail to the northward where the prizes were more plentiful and easier to take.

One of the strangest pirates to cruise off the Virginia coast, and indeed, one of the strangest of all times, was one who originally held the rank and name of Major Stede Bonnet. He was of a good English family, and was himself considered "a gentleman that has had the Advantage of a liberal Education, and being generally esteemed a Man of Letters." Of middle age, he had every reason to settle down and enjoy the life of a successful planter. His sugar plantation brought him wealth and he enjoyed the company of the best society of Bridgetown on the island of Barbados.

Suddenly, and for no apparent reason, Major Bonnet turned from gentleman planter to pirate, scandalizing his neighbors who excused the action on the grounds that the likeable major was suffering some "Disorder in his Mind," a speculation that might well have been true. There were some who suggested that his disaffection with respectability was the result of the nagging tongue of a shrewish wife, along with "some Discomforts he found in the married state."

As a pirate, Stede Bonnet was strictly an amateur. Rather than steal or capture a ship as any self-respecting pirate might do, he purchased his own vessel, something almost unheard of in the annals of piracy. This fast little sloop, purchased in early 1717, had ten artillery pieces lashed to her single gun deck. For no obvious reason he renamed her the *Revenge*. Rather than drawing up articles for his crew to sign, Bonnet did an equally unheard of thing, by paying them wages out of his own pocket. It was through this maneuver, however, that he could remain in command of the ship and could not be deposed by the crew—unless they mutinied. From the taverns and grogshops of Bridgetown he signed on some seventy derelict seamen.

For several days the *Revenge* lay rocking gently in the quiet waters of Bridgetown harbor. To the curious, Bonnet gave out the story that he had purchased the sloop to work up an inter-island trade. Then, one dark night, without a word of farewell to his friends or the whining Mrs. Bonnet, he upped anchor and slipped over the Bridgetown bar into the open Atlantic. Once out of sight of land he set a course for the Virginia capes.

Bonnet captured several vessels off the capes, although the name of only one is recorded. This was the sloop, *Turbes,* out of Barbados. The other prizes were only plundered and then released, but the *Turbes* was burned, thereby establishing a pattern. From this time on, every Barbadian ship taken by Bonnet was burned, almost as if he were attempting to cremate his past.

Sailing north, the *Revenge* took several prizes off the New England coast, and Bonnet discovered there was a ready market for pirate booty in New York. But hunting was not too good in northern waters and, after stopping off Long Island to take on provisions, he returned to the south. Bonnet hove to off Charleston and almost immediately took a brigantine and a sloop. The brigantine was released, but the sloop, from Barbados with a cargo of "sugar rum and Negroes," was retained, although the crew were allowed to make their way to safety. Turning north again, Bonnet slipped into an obscure inlet on the North Carolina coast. The Barbadian sloop was burned, after which the *Revenge* was careened and her hull scraped clean of parasitic growth.

With his ship slipping cleanly through the water again, Bonnet cleared the North Carolina coast and sailed for the Bay of Honduras. Trouble was brewing. The captain's inexperience had become obvious, and the crew were becoming surly and whispering amongst themselves. Stern disciplinary measures were imposed, but by the time Bonnet dropped anchor in the Bay of Honduras, the grumblings had steadily increased.

It was in the Bay of Honduras that Bonnet met up with the *Queen Anne's Revenge,* and her captain, the fearsome person who delighted in the nickname of "Blackbeard," rather than his true name, Edward Teach. This strange pair of captains, the amateur and the veteran, struck up a friendship and decided to cruise together. Shortly afterwards they headed out to sea.

Teach was soon aware that "he had caught an odd sort of fish." Friendship waned as Bonnet's lack of knowledge in the ways of the sea became evident. Bonnet was invited over to the *Queen Anne's Revenge,* and from the moment he stepped on deck he became a virtual prisoner. Teach flattered him with the observation that a man of his education and genteel manners should not be forced to undergo the rigors of command. It was much better, he said, that the major should take his ease in the more comfortable and spacious quarters aboard the *Queen Anne's Revenge.* There was little that Bonnet could do or say other than reproach himself for being so great a fool as to ally himself with the more powerful leader. One of Blackbeard's lieutenants, Richards by name, was sent over to command the *Revenge.* There was no longer a threat of mutiny aboard the sloop as Richards imposed a stern discipline and gained the confidence of the crew.

The ships plied the sea lanes between the Bahamas and the Carolinas; at least twelve prizes were taken. Several were converted to pirate use to accommodate the large number of seamen among the prisoners who expressed a desire to join the pirate gang. Although still allowed a captain's share in the booty, Bonnet sulked in shame in his cabin aboard the *Queen Anne's Revenge.* By the time that Teach set sail for North Carolina, he was something of a pirate admiral, having under his command a little fleet of four ships and no fewer than 140 men.

Teach's command arrived in North Carolina's Topsail Inlet in June, 1718. Two of the ships were run aground in shallow water. Tensions mounted as the pirates began to quarrel among themselves. As dissensions swelled, Teach informed Bonnet that he was free to take over command of the *Revenge* again.

Bonnet seems to have grown weary of the pirate life. Yet, according to some with whom he talked, he gave the impression that he would be ashamed to see the face of an Englishman again, and if he could but get away he would retire to Spain or Portugal and there live under an assumed name. Perhaps this is the reason that he decided to seek the King's mercy under the royal proclamation. He also learned that war had broken out between the Triple Alliance and Spain. This not only would allow him forgiveness for his transgressions of the past, but it was possible that he might further his career as a privateer. Leaving his ship, he hastened over to the town of Bath and there surrendered himself as a reformed pirate to Governor Charles Eden of North Carolina. The governor granted him permission to sail to St. Thomas in the Virgin Islands to secure for himself a commission as a privateer.

Returning to Topsail Inlet, Bonnet found that Blackbeard had betrayed his former shipmates. The *Revenge* was safely anchored, but the other two vessels had been run aground while Teach had put out to sea with all the plunder, including that belonging to Bonnet and his men. He had likewise stripped the sloop of all arms and provisions, and had selected fourteen of the better seamen from the *Revenge* and sent them aboard his own vessel. The remaining twenty-five he considered superfluous and marooned them on a sand bar that was barely above water at high tide and where there was "neither Bird, Beast, nor Herb." He had left them with no food and water. Only five hands were still aboard the *Revenge*.

There is little doubt but that Bonnet, his quartermaster, and his boatswain had schemed to return to pirating just as soon as the "Act of Grace" had been granted by Governor Eden. In his absence the *Revenge* had been rerigged to give her greater speed. The men marooned by Teach escaped a lonely death when Bonnet rescued them after they had been on the sand spit for two days and two nights. Several others who had fled from Teach were discovered in nearby settlements on the mainland. Bonnet's crew, when finally assembled, was composed of ten Englishmen, nine West Indians, five Scotsmen, four from North Carolina, three from South Carolina, two Irishmen, and a Dutchman. He told them that he was sailing for St. Thomas to seek the "Emperor's Commission," and requested that they join him as privateers. Small boats began to bring out provisions. From one of these, laden with "apples and cider to sell," it was learned that Teach, with a crew of only eighteen, was anchored in Ocracoke Inlet. Bonnet did not wait until his sloop was fully provisioned. Piling on sail, he headed for Ocracoke, but was thwarted in his desire for retribution. Teach, he was told, had sailed northward just a few hours earlier.

It was useless to continue the pursuit of Teach without adequate provisions, but Bonnet assured his crew that "he should go on the Coast of Virginia to see for some." Sailing out of Ocracoke, all pretenses of privateering were abandoned as they hoisted the "bloody Flag." There is some testimony given in Bonnet's trial to suggest that his crew forced him to return to the life of a pirate, and that he went so far as to offer to leave them and go ashore and allow them to continue as they pleased. On the other hand, any resistance that he offered must have been weak, for from this time on a streak of cruelty underlies Bonnet's character. Yet, when they overtook a small ship shortly after leaving Ocracoke, and took from it bread and pork, Bonnet reimbursed the captain for his loss. But the next three victims, all sloops from Bermuda, were scuttled and the crews set ashore.

Several changes had taken place, perhaps because Bonnet wished to cloud reports of his activities after having accepted the King's pardon. He now referred to himself as "Captain Thomas," and the name of the sloop was changed from the *Revenge* to the *Royal James,* a suggestion of the Jacobean leanings of one who supported the return of the Stuarts to the throne of England. As in the past, however, the captain began to lose the confidence of his crew. Robert Hunter of Jamaica was elected quarter-master, and it was later testified that he exercised more authority than did Bonnet.

A slave ship was captured, and the pick of the cargo was dispatched to a safe slave market to be auctioned off. Several sloops were taken off the capes of Virginia, one of which they plundered of thirty barrels of beef, some butter, and other provisions. Bonnet either felt kindly toward the captain, or his storage space was becoming limited, for he made the captain a present of a number of barrels of molasses as a partial compensation for his loss. Out of other prizes he claimed tobacco and provisions. In all, Bonnet captured thirteen prizes between Cape Fear and Delaware Bay, at least six of which were taken off Virginia.

Two vessels taken during this voyage were responsible, ultimately, for the doom of the crew of the *Royal James*. On August 5, 1718, two miles off Cape James (also known as Cape Henlopen), Captain Peter Mainwaring's *Francis* was boarded. It was an easy conquest. The *Francis* lay anchored and made no attempt to defend herself when Bonnet sent over a dory filled with pirates. Mainwaring stated that when he came aboard the *Royal James* the pirates clapped their hands to their cutlasses and said, "they would [be kind] if we were Civil." They were, continued Mainwaring, "civil to me, very civil: But they were all brisk and merry and had all Things plentiful, and were a-making Punch and drinking." The punch, incidentally, was made from pineapples taken from one of the West Indian sloops, and the crew "went to drinking the Pretender's Health and hoped to see him King of the English Nation."

The other vessel whose capture was destined to play a role in Bonnet's trial was the merchant sloop *Fortune,* Captain Thomas Read, taken off Cape Fear. Some of the prisoners they took along to help sail their prizes; others, including a woman identified as "Reeve's Wife," and Captain Read's son were sent ashore. The captains were kept aboard, possibly with some intention of using them as hostages should the situation grow critical.

The *Royal James* was beginning to leak and was badly in need of careening. Enough cordage and sails had been taken from prizes for a general overhaul of the sloop. A course was set for the Cape Fear River, where the maze of wandering waterways near the mouth of the river provided a convenient site for careening ships. The danger was lessened in that Governor Eden was fast gaining a reputation as a friend of the freebooters.

The *Royal James* was in worse shape than had been anticipated. Repairs, it was estimated, would take the better part of two months. In their haste to make their craft seaworthy in the least possible time, Bonnet and his crew became careless. A shallop was captured and broken up, its lumber to be used in making repairs. A mistake was made in releasing the crew of the prize; they spread the word that a pirate ship was laid up in the lower Cape Fear.

By this time the people of Charleston and South Carolina were growing weary of being bullied by every tramp pirate who happened by. Governor Robert Johnson, well aware that he would receive little cooperation from Governor Eden, planned to rid himself of at least one of these pests, although the colony's finances were feeble because of recent Indian wars. Colonel William Rhett, receiver-general of South Carolina, offered his services as a leader, and proper authorizations were issued. Two sloops, the *Sea Nymph* and the *Henry,* each mounting eighteen guns, were pressed into service. Seventy-six men made up the crew of the *Henry,* while the smaller *Sea Nymph* could accommodate but fifty-six.

Provisions, arms, and ammunition were being taken aboard when a sloop out of Antigua scurried into Charleston harbor. The infamous Charles Vane, her captain reported, had stopped him on the far side of the bar and plundered his cargo, along with those of two other ships. Vane, he said, commanded a brigantine manned by a crew of ninety. The pirate captain had been overheard to say that he intended dropping down south of Charleston to make repairs to his brigantine. Vane, long a thorn in the side of the Charlestonians, became a more immediate concern than the unknown pirate in the Cape Fear. The expedition took on the air of a crusade. Colonel Rhett "went in Person, accompanied by many Gentlemen of the Town, animated with the same Principle of Zeal and Honour for our public Safety, and the Preservation of Trade." A futile search was conducted south of Charleston before Rhett learned that Vane had sailed northward.

On the chance that the pirate in the Cape Fear might be Vane, Rhett set a course for the mouth of that river. On September 28, 1718, the two sloops beat their way into the Cape Fear. There had been no time to pick up a pilot, and they soon ran aground in the unfamiliar waters.

They were in sight of the enemy. Even before they ran aground the topmasts of the *Royal James* could be seen, silhouetted above the trees on a point of land farther upstream. High tide would not refloat Rhett's sloops before midnight, and it would have been dangerous to attempt a night attack in shoal waters. As they waited, Rhett cleared the decks for the action that would come with sunrise.

It was almost sundown when the pirates discovered their presence; the gathering dusk made it impossible to determine whether they were potential prizes or an enemy. Bonnet sent out two small boats to investigate the strangers. They returned with the unhappy news that the two sloops were heavily armed and carried a full complement of men. Bonnet drove his men in putting the *Royal James* in fighting trim. Sometime during the night he went below and addressed an angry letter to Governor Johnson; if he came out of this fight alive, he raged, he would plunder and burn every ship that had the temerity to sail out of Charleston harbor. Then, his wrath eased, he returned to the deck to drive his men.

Dawn broke. Both Bonnet and Rhett were ready for battle. There was a rattle of anchor chains and the sigh of the breeze in the sails as the pirates prepared to carry the fight to the enemy. Bonnet had devised a simple strategy: to force Rhett into a running fight and then bull his way through into the open sea where there was a greater opportunity to maneuver—and escape should it become necessary.

Rhett anticipated such a move. Anchors were weighed as the *Henry* and the *Sea Nymph* came in, attempting to force the *Royal James* into the shallow water near the shore. All three ships kept up an almost continuous cannonade. In the beginning, Rhett's maneuvers appeared to be meeting with success. The pirate vessel shuddered to a stop on a sand bank. The attackers moved in, maneuvering too quickly and too recklessly as both sloops ground to a halt in the shallows of the river. Not for another five hours would the tide refloat the three ships.

The *Sea Nymph,* attempting to block the flight of the pirate into the open sea, ran aground too far downstream to play any important role in the immediate future. The *Henry,* on the other hand, was within pistol range of the *Royal James.* Both ships listed at the same angle, leaving Bonnet's men protected while exposing the crew of the *Henry* to the fire of the pirates. Despite the rain of iron, Rhett's men managed to bring some of their guns to bear on the *Royal James.* Balls began to crash through the hull of Bonnet's sloop.

Still the pirates were jubilant, confident that victory would be theirs. During lulls in the firing, they shouted taunts across the open water, inviting Rhett's men to pay them a visit—if they dared. At the same time they impudently made a "a Wiff in their bloody Flag." The crew of the *Henry* replied with "cheerful huzzas," promising they would soon come aboard, and much too soon for the comfort of the pirates.

The tide turned! All three sloops held fast. Then, as the water deepened beneath her hull, the *Henry* slowly righted herself. The men relieved their tensions with a lusty "Hurrah!" The will to fight waned aboard the *Royal James* as the enemy became seaborne. The pirate crew crowded around their captain, demanding that they surrender. Bonnet, his temper blazing, swore that he would blow up the ship rather than give in and, brandishing his pistols, shouted that he would blow out the brains of any man who refused to fight to the last.

This heated exchange consumed time. Rhett used the lull to make hasty repairs to his ship. His sloop seaworthy, he steered for the *Royal James,* planning to bear in tight and board the enemy. Bonnet's flag fluttered down in surrender. For the next few minutes there was an attempt to negotiate in shouts across the water. Bonnet, on gaining Rhett's promise that he would intercede in an attempt to gain mercy, agreed to surrender. Only then did Rhett discover that Captain Thomas was the more notorious Stede Bonnet.

The fight had lasted for more than six hours. It had not been an easy

The capture of Stede Bonnet.

victory. On board the *Henry,* ten men had been killed and fourteen wounded, some of whom later died. Before she had been forced out of the engagement, the *Sea Nymph* had suffered casualties of two killed and four wounded. On the *Royal James,* seven pirates lay dead, with another five wounded. Thirty-five prisoners were taken, three of whom later died of their wounds.

On October 3, 1718, Rhett and his prize limped back into Charleston harbor "to the great joy of the whole Province." The prisoners created a problem, for Charleston had no jail that could accommodate so many. The pirate crew was placed under heavy guard in the public watchhouse. Bonnet, considered a gentleman by birth and education, was not to be thrown in with common criminals. The major was placed in the custody of the town marshal, who furnished Bonnet lodgings in his own house. Several days later, two other crew members from the *Royal James,* David Herriot, sailing master, and Ignatius Pell, boatswain, were also placed in the marshal's house. Both had agreed to turn King's evidence, and they were separated from their former shipmates lest they suffer bodily harm.

The trial was scheduled within the next four weeks, allowing the Assembly ample time to introduce and pass "An Act for the more speedy and regular trial of pirates." Bonnet, however, had influential friends, perhaps those who had dealt with the pirates in the past and now wished to remove the possibility of damaging revelations. Others were not sure that he should be hanged as a pirate, a view perhaps best noted in a later statement by Attorney General Richard Allein: "I am sorry to hear some Expressions drop from private Persons in favor of Pirates, and particularly of Bonnet; that he is a Gentleman, a Man of Honour, a Man of Fortune and one that has had a liberal Education. Alas, Gentlemen, all of these Qualifications are but several Aggravations of his Crimes."

Gold was offered the two sentinels posted at the marshal's house. On October 25, three days before the trial, Stede Bonnet and David Herriot escaped. Some say Bonnet slipped away dressed in the clothes of a woman. Ignatius Pell preferred to remain and take his chances on a pardon in return for the evidence he was to give. A £700 reward was placed on Bonnet's head. Colonel Rhett was given command of the *posse comitatus* organized to pursue the escaped pirates.

A small boat had been waiting for Bonnet, as were several men who wished to join the major should he go a-pirating again. They attempted to flee into the more congenial surroundings of North Carolina, but contrary winds forced them back. Stealing into Charleston harbor, they took refuge on Sullivan's Island, just a few miles from Charleston and almost diagonally across the bay.

Their whereabouts was soon known. On November 6, Rhett waited until after darkness had set in before landing on the island. Hours were spent searching through the palmettos and low myrtle bushes that clung to the dunes. When Bonnet's camp was discovered near the upper end of the island, Rhett's men opened fire without warning. Herriot was killed at the first fire. A Negro and an Indian who had joined Bonnet suffered severe wounds. Bonnet surrendered without resistance. Taken to Charleston, he was placed under a heavy guard. That same day, two large ships were taken by pirates within sight of the town.

While Bonnet was at large, his crew had been brought to trial before the vice-admiralty court in Charleston on October 28, 1718. Nicholas Trott, a cousin of the former West Indian governor and the presiding judge, held a reputation as a magistrate of little mercy. Every prisoner entered a plea of not guilty, and to a man claimed that they had been forced into piracy against their wills. Ignatius Pell, fighting for his life, gave the lie to their pleas. Captains Mainwaring and Read testified for the prosecution. There was little doubt as to the eventual outcome; of late Charleston had suffered too many indignities at the hands of pirates to be inclined to mercy. All of Bonnet's crew, with the exception of Ignatius Pell and three others who were able to prove that they had been forced, were found guilty. In a solemn address, sprinkled with biblical phrases, Judge Trott pronounced their doom.

On November 8, 1718, the twenty-nine condemned men were taken down to White Point and there were hanged on the gallows at the water's edge. In their last statements, many of those whom Bonnet had "seduced" into a life of crime, "with their last Breath expressed a great Satisfaction of the Prisoner's being apprehended, and charged the Ruin of themselves and the Loss of their Lives entirely upon him." As a deterrent to those adventurous souls who might be inclined to take up similar careers, they were left hanging and "dancing in the four winds" for several days. They were then cut down to be buried below the high water mark at the edge of the marsh.

Two days after this gruesome spectacle on White Point, Stede Bonnet was brought to trial. As expected, he pleaded not guilty, and attempted to charm those witnesses who testified against him. But he could muster no real defense. On November 12, Judge Trott, in his summation, reviewed Bonnet's checkered past and predicted that Bonnet would suffer all the tortures of Hell "in the lake which burneth with fire and brimstone, which is the second death." And then came the awful words: "That you the said Stede Bonnet shall go from hence to the Place from whence you came, and from thence to the Place of Execution, where you shall be hanged by the Neck till you are Dead. And the God of infinite Mercy be merciful to your Soul."

Governor Johnson designated Wednesday, December 10, as the date of the execution. Stede Bonnet, former soldier and bold pirate, now became a groveling shadow of a man, living out his remaining days in abject terror and agony. Yet there were those who worked in his behalf, including William Rhett who was living up to his promise that he would attempt to intercede for mercy. Petitions to the governor requested that the pirate captain be either pardoned or have his sentence commuted, or even that he be sent to England where his case might be reviewed by the proper authorities. Rhett offered to accompany the former pirate to England in an attempt to gain a new trial should the governor give his consent.

Johnson was obdurate in the face of the weaknesses of those who had in the past cried out so passionately against the ravages of pirates. A few days before the execution, the tremulous Bonnet addressed one last plea to the governor. In pious terror he wrote:

I once more beg for the Lord's sake, dear sir, that as you are a Christian, you will be as charitable as to have Mercy and Compassion on my miserable Soul, but too newly awakened from an Habit of Sin to entertain so confident Hopes and Assurances of my blessed Jesus, as is necessary to reconcile me to so speedy a Death; wherefore as my Life, Blood, Reputation of my Family, and future happy State lies entirely at your Disposal, I implore you to consider me with a Christian and charitable Heart, and determine mercifully of me that I may ever acknowledge and esteem you next to God, my Saviour; and oblige me ever to pray that our heavenly Father will also forgive your Trespasses.

The governor stood steadfast. On December 10, Bonnet was brought down to White Point in a state of near collapse, with one observer noting that "he was scarce sensible when he came to the place of execution." A few minutes later, his manacled hands clasping the traditional nosegay of flowers, Stede Bonnet was "swung off" the cart beneath the gallows into eternity. After his body was cut down, it was taken down to the edge of the marsh and buried near the bodies of those men he had led to their doom.

Stede Bonnet's life had been an unhappy one, both as a gentleman and as a pirate. In both roles he had displayed a psychotic weakness that had made him fit for neither.

VI

BLACKBEARD, SPAWN OF THE DEVIL

"Damnation seize my Soul if I give you Quarters!"

Pirates seldom wandered within the Virginia capes during 1717, but they engaged in much activity in the open seas off the coast. Many of the dangers of the past were eliminated with the arrival of two well-equipped frigates, the *Lyme* and the *Pearl*. Arriving in August, 1717, the *Lyme* did not renew the practice of pressing seamen, for she had a full complement of 111 "healthy" seamen.

Despite the presence of the frigates, there was a constant flow of rumors about pirates who were operating, or who soon would be operating, in these waters. Captain Ellis Brand of the *Lyme* was irritated when many ships, hailed by a strange vessel, piled on all sail and raced into the bay, proclaiming to all that they had been chased by pirates. To the contrary, Brand felt that the proclamation of the King offering forgiveness for past transgressions was having a salutary effect on the actions of the freebooters. In fact, he reported that during the interval between August, 1717, and May, 1718, he had heard of but one pirate ship and that was off the Delaware capes. Brand had not been on the Virginia station long enough to realize that in the period of which he spoke the pirates sought a warmer climate.

◄ Blackbeard, as he was depicted in the original edition of Johnson's *A General History of the Pirates,* 1724.

105

In fact, in Virginia, the proclamation did appear to be effective. Pirates, some from as far away as New Providence, came into Virginia to accept the royal pardon. Some remained in the colony and appear to have been accepted into local society without too much prejudice so long as they spent freely the hard money they brought with them. Others accepted the pardon with a penitent air—and almost immediately began to scheme of ways to gain another ship and take up "the sport again." By early 1718 twenty pirate vessels were reported operating between Virginia and South Carolina, some lately of New Providence whence they had fled when Woodes Rogers broke up their pirate republic. The presence of guard ships, however, kept many at a safe distance. It was now possible to careen one of the frigates without exposing local trade to the freebooters. The threat was further diminished when the Virginia guard ships received excellent cooperation from Captain Pierce of the *Phoenix,* the guard ship stationed in New York. The only real menace during the winter of 1717–1718 was from Captain Edward Teach who was reported, from time to time, to be operating off the Virginia capes.

The origins of Edward Teach are obscure. There is some doubt that his true name was Teach; contemporary accounts refer to him as Thatch, Tache, Tatch, and even Tash, although he was usually spoken of as "Captain Thatch, alias Blackbeard." There is one suggestion that his true name may have been Hyde. Yet in the official records he is always known as Thatch or Teach. By many it has been accepted that he was born Edward Drummond in Bristol, England, although some early North Carolina historians state that he was born in Accomac County on the Eastern Shore of Virginia. Still another account has him born in Jamaica of "very creditable parents." Yet it was as Blackbeard that he became feared by the honest seafarers of colonial America, who knew him as "a swaggering merciless brute."

If indeed his name was Drummond and he did spend his early life in Bristol, the environment there might have been responsible for his later career, for Bristol turned out more pirates in the seventeenth and eighteenth centuries than any other English port. It seems that he originally shipped out as a merchant seaman, and his introduction to piracy came aboard a privateer sailing out of Kingston, Jamaica, during the later years of Queen Anne's War.

By the time the war ended, or perhaps earlier, he was calling himself Edward Teach. Restlessness came with peace, and Teach signed the articles of the company under the command of Captain Benjamin Hornigold. Hornigold's brigantine, the *Ranger,* mounted thirty-six guns and carried at least 145 men in the company. In this large crew, Teach created a coterie of followers. The man seems to have had a natural bent for leadership, and early distinguished himself by his strength, raw courage, and something of a devil-may-care attitude. Only a little time had passed before his abilities were recognized and he was placed in command of a six-gun sloop and about seventy men, sailing in consort with the *Ranger.*

On a voyage off the North American coast in late 1716, Hornigold careened and repaired the *Ranger* on the Virginia coast after he had taken a large number of prizes. It was during this cruise that Edward Teach got his first real opportunity to become an independent pirate captain. Near the island of St. Vincent in the West Indies, a French ship, the *Concorde* of St. Malo, was captured and plundered of Negroes, gold dust, money, plate, and jewels. Well-built and fast, this prize presented to Teach the opportunity to realize his own ambitions. Collecting those who seemed inclined to accept his leadership, Teach went to Hornigold and requested that he be allowed to assume command of the *Concorde* and convert her into a pirate ship. When Hornigold granted this request, Teach was well on his way to becoming a legend in the annals of piracy.

Both ships made for New Providence. In Nassau they were offered the opportunity of accepting the terms of the royal proclamation. Hornigold, a man of some wealth, and weary of the uncertain life of a pirate, surrendered himself and claimed the mercy of the Crown. Shortly afterwards he returned to sea as an agent of Woodes Rogers in chasing down his former colleagues. The majority of his crew followed Hornigold's example: about fifty surrendered to the governor of Jamaica, twenty to the governors of Rhode Island and New York, others went into New England and South Carolina, while at least eight came into Virginia to surrender.

Teach entertained no idea of spending the rest of his years in peace and oblivion. Mounting forty guns on his new command, he christened her the *Queen Anne's Revenge;* she was more than a match for the largest and best armed of merchant vessels. The *Queen Anne's Revenge,* it was said, was "as well outfitted with warlike Stores of all Sorts as any Fifth-Rate Ship in the Navy." He entered upon his new command in grand style. Soon after leaving New Providence, he captured a large English merchantman, the *Great Allan,* off St. Vincent. Transferring the more valuable items of the cargo to his own hold, he set the crew ashore and put the *Great Allan* to the torch.

With the news of this capture of an English ship, the thirty-gun frigate *Scarborough* put out to sea in search of the *Queen Anne's Revenge.* When the pirate ship was sighted, the naval vessel closed in for the kill. Teach, unlike most pirate captains, was ready and willing to fight and exchanged broadsides with the *Scarborough.* After a bloody engagement lasting for several hours, the out-gunned *Scarborough* drew off and limped her crestfallen way back into the nearest port. The news that Teach had fought and driven off a frigate of the Royal Navy did nothing to lessen his reputation.

It was about this time that Teach began to cultivate the use of the name "Blackbeard." He seemed to know instinctively which features of his physical makeup should be accentuated. He was tall for the age he lived in, and powerful of physique. It was from his long, bushy beard that he received his name; one eighteenth century writer described it as a "large Quantity of Hair which, like a frightful Meteor, covered his whole Face, and frightened America more than any Comet that has appeared there for a long Time."

Teach allowed his beard to grow untrimmed; it was long and rose on his face almost to the level of his eyes. He was wont to plait the beard into little tails, the ends of which he tied with fanciful colored ribbons. Some of these braids he twisted back over his ears. Before an impending engagement, he exaggerated an already frightful appearance by tucking slow-burning matches under his hat, wreathing his face in wispy curls of smoke, as if he were the Devil himself, fresh from Hell's outer reaches. Preparatory to action, he swung a bandolier over his shoulders containing three braces of pistols, loaded, primed, and cocked for instant firing. In a wide belt around his waist were additional pistols, daggers, and a cutlass. All in all, he was a most awesome sight, a seafaring ogre whose reputation withered the courage of brave men.

Sometime in May, 1717, not too long after his encounter with the

Scarborough, Teach sailed for the Bay of Honduras, a southern rendezvous for pirates. It was there that he met Stede Bonnet, and it was there
that he made Bonnet a virtual prisoner, "telling him that as he had not
been used to the Fatigues and Care of such a Post, it would be better for
him to decline it and live easy at his Pleasure."

Teach's *Queen Anne's Revenge* and Bonnet's *Revenge* made a good
working pair. They took a number of prizes in the West Indies, and the
name of Blackbeard became so feared that the governor of the Leeward
Islands demanded an armed escort when he sailed from one island to
another.

In January, 1718, Teach sailed the two ships into North Carolina. At the
town of Bath he surrendered to Governor Charles Eden under the terms
of the current Act of Grace. This surrender was little more than a
formality, and seems to have been more in the nature of an insurance
policy than anything else. The act was accomplished with the connivance
of the governor, and the pirates openly prepared for another voyage,
making little or no attempt to conceal their intentions. Tobias Knight,
secretary of the colony and collector of customs, was as deeply involved as
the governor, if not more so. It was through the cooperation of these two
executives that Blackbeard and his crew were allowed to maintain what
amounted to a protected base of operations on the North American
mainland. Bath was an excellent base, with good careening sites in the
vicinity, friendly officials, and merchants eager to purchase pirate plunder
with few or no questions asked.

They sailed once again for the Bay of Honduras. Off Turniffe Island
they hove to in order to fill their water casks. As they lay at anchor, a
sloop was sighted beating its way into shore for the same purpose.
Quickly slipping his cable, Richards in the *Revenge* overhauled the
stranger. The sloop, the *Adventure* out of Jamaica, hauled down her flag
without resistance. Her master, David Herriot (who was to be killed
when Bonnet was recaptured after his jail break) joined the rest of his
crew in signing the pirate articles of Teach's company. Israel Hands,
sometimes called Hezekiah or Basilica Hands, was given command of the
Adventure.

There was good hunting in the Bay of Honduras. A Boston ship, the
Protestant Caesar and four sloops were discovered lying at anchor. The

sight of the Jolly Roger so frightened the crews that they scrambled over the sides into small boats and pulled for the safety of the shore. Inasmuch as the people of Boston had but recently hanged a number of pirates, the *Protestant Caesar* and a sloop from New England were burned. One of the remaining sloops was added to the pirate squadron.

Teach now commanded a fleet of pirate ships: the *Queen Anne's Revenge*, Bonnet's *Revenge*, and the *Adventure*, along with the newest sloop and several small tenders. The total number of men aboard numbered near 400. They haunted the sea lanes between the West Indies and the mainland. Several of those Barbadian sloops taken were burned, perhaps to satisfy Bonnet's personal vendetta against all things of Barbados. Several times they put in to Havana to dispose of their plunder. Still North Carolina remained something of a rendezvous for the group. As it was dangerous to follow any established pattern of behavior, they used a number of hideouts including the Cape Fear and the Chowan Rivers, but their favorite refuge seems to have been Ocracoke Inlet, where tradition says that a house known as "Blackbeard's Castle" used to stand in the village. One cove, where the pirate came to careen his ships, is still known as "Teach's hole."

Teach was a man determined to keep his evil image alive. He drank heavily, as did the majority of his crew. According to one source, a fragment of his journal, "found writ with his own Hand," ran:

"such a Day—Rum all out—Our Company somewhat sober:—A damn'd Confusion amongst us!—Rogues a plotting;—great Talk of Separation.—So I look'd Sharp for a Prize."

The next entry stated:

"such a Day took one, with a great deal of Liquor on Board, so kept the Company hot, damned hot, then all Things went well again."

One day, while becalmed on a flat and glassy sea, the men grew irritable and were drinking heavily from the rum barrels. The captain, "a little flushed with drink," suddenly shouted to those around him that they should join him in making "a Hell of our own, and try how long we can bear it." Three of the more daring members of the company accepted the challenge and followed Teach down into the hold. They sat down on the large stones used as ballast. The captain roared an order that several large pots of burning brimstone be brought down. The hatches were battened tight. The dank hold was soon filled with swirling clouds of choking, sulfurous fumes, but only after the challengers cried for air were the hatches opened. They were followed up to the deck by a grinning Teach, not a little pleased that he had held out the longest. One of the crew, it was said, had the temerity to cry out, "Why Captain, you look as if you were coming straight from the gallows." "My lad," cried the captain, "that's a brilliant idea. The next time we shall play at gallows and see who can swing longest on the string without being throttled." There were no challengers to this proposal.

This man Blackbeard held strange ideas as to the proper methods for maintaining discipline. One night, drinking in his cabin with Israel Hands and another member of the crew, Teach suddenly drew two pistols, cocked them and thrust the weapons beneath the table. He blew out the candle. Hands did not move, but his companion fled from the cabin. Crossing his hands beneath the table, Teach fired both pistols. Israel Hands received the full charge of one pistol in his knee, an injury that was to leave him lame for the rest of his life. When others asked why he would intentionally injure a man he called friend, the captain explained that "if he did not now and then kill one of them, they would forget who he was."

In May 1718, Teach and his flotilla lay off Charleston harbor. Almost immediately three prizes were taken, all laden with rich cargoes. One ship was carrying fourteen prime slaves, while £1,500 in gold was discovered aboard another. Five or six smaller craft, unaware of the danger on the far side of the bar, sailed out and were promptly captured. By this time, news of the pirates outside the harbor filtered back into Charleston. Trade came to a standstill. Eight or nine ships ready for sea lay at the wharves, not daring to hoist their sails and put out to sea.

One of the prizes must have resisted, or there was a sudden outbreak of sickness among the pirates, for they suddenly found themselves in need of medical supplies. Aboard one of their prizes, outward bound for London, had been four passengers, including Samuel Wragg, a member of Governor Johnson's council. Wragg and his four year old son, William, were held as hostages. Richards, the commander of the *Revenge*, along with

three or four other pirates, was sent in to Charleston to demand medi-
cines as ransom for Wragg and the other prisoners. One of the passengers,
a Mr. Marks, was sent in with them to verify the facts of the story.

Richards delivered Blackbeard's insolent demand to the governor. Unless the pirates' medical chest was replenished within two days, the
hostages would be murdered and their heads delivered to Johnson. A
delay would mean that Teach would "burn the ships that lay before the
town and beat it about our ears."

The governor and his council met in emergency session. While they
deliberated, Richards and his companions strutted arrogantly and boldly
about the town. There was nothing for the governor to do but suppress
his pride and give in to the pirates. There was no guard ship in Charleston and, had he so desired, Teach could have sailed into the harbor and
battered the shipping and waterfront as he had threatened. With humilia-
tion and embarrassment, governor and council gathered together medical
supplies worth £300 to £400.

Still holding Marks as a hostage, Richard started back to the ships. A
sudden squall capsized their small boat and forced them back to shore.
They could not reach the *Queen Anne's Revenge* until the two-day
deadline had expired, but Blackbeard had not carried into execution his
threat to murder the hostages. They were released, but not until they had
been plucked clean. The prisoners were relieved of all their money,
including £6,000 found on Samuel Wragg. They were stripped of their
finery and sent ashore, half naked. As the pirates set their sails for North
Carolina, they left behind an angry citizenry, inclined neither to forgive
nor forget, as Stede Bonnet and his crew were to discover.

It was June, 1718, when Teach and his crew reached Topsail Inlet in
North Carolina. Since April 5, he and Bonnet had taken at least twenty-
eight prizes in the West Indies and off the southern mainland colonies. As
they steered into the inlet, on a pretense of careening, the *Queen Anne's
Revenge* and one of the sloops coming to her aid ran aground. This
grounding was a deliberate act on the part of the pirate captain, for the
number of men under his command had grown so great that the share-
outs were small. Some of the crew were growing restless and two factions
had sprung up among them. One of these groups, it was whispered,

wanted to depose the captain. The situation had grown so tense that there was a great danger of the two parties fighting each other.

With a great show of generosity, Teach allowed Bonnet to assume command of the *Revenge* once again. Then he persuaded him to travel overland to Bath to seek the Act of Grace from Governor Eden. Bonnet was no sooner out of sight than Teach loaded all the plunder, ammunition, and supplies aboard the *Adventure,* which Teach considered to be the better ship for the smaller crew. A sizeable number of the 320 whites and Negroes under his command were dismissed. Some fled to escape the wrath of their former captain. When those who remained objected to his methods, they were marooned on a lonely sand bar, where Stede Bonnet ultimately found them. Teach, with forty selected crewmen, including Israel Hands, put out to sea. Some of those left behind made their way into the interior of North Carolina, some went to Virginia, while still others traveled overland to Philadelphia and New York. At least twenty seem to have refloated their grounded sloop and returned to their profession, although "pretending to Employ themselves in Trade."

Soon after the breakup of his former command, Teach sailed to Bath where he once again surrendered to Governor Eden who, illegally and without question, granted the King's mercy to the pirate captain and twenty of his men. The governor also convened a "pretended Court of Admiralty," with Tobias Knight presiding as chief justice and solemnly condemned the *Adventure* as a lawful Spanish prize, even though England and Spain were not at war with each other at the time. Blackbeard was allowed to retain full ownership of the sloop, although apparently not without assuring the governor and the secretary that they would share in all future spoils. It was such a flouting of proper legal procedures that the High Court of Admiralty in London suggested that in the future all prizes be brought to London for condemnation rather than in the colonial courts, "since it is too much to be feared that they are not well versed in the Laws of Nations, and the Treaties between us and other states, and it is well known that they do not proceed in that regular manner as it is practised in His Majesty's High Court of Admiralty."

Blackbeard sailed forth on a rather extensive voyage. At one time his men were reported walking about the streets of Philadelphia, and in

August, 1718, Governor William Keith of Pennsylvania issued a warrant for Teach's arrest. When the pirates returned to Bath, they had as prisoners some eighty or ninety Negroes, whom they claimed were from a French vessel and, with the connivance of the local authorities, were sold into slavery as legitimate prizes. It was later discovered that the Negroes had been taken from an English vessel.

About this time romance re-entered the life of the bearded pirate captain. He bought himself a fine home. His lavish display of fine silks, jewels, and gold so addled the brain of one sixteen-year-old lass that she consented to become his wife. One contemporary commented, "and this, I have been informed, made Teach's fourteenth Wife, whereof a dozen might still be living." It was rumored that the pirate's primary purpose in matrimony was "to put a gloss to his designs." The governor himself attended the wedding; some reports suggest that he actually performed the ceremony. The latest Mrs. Teach was soon to regret her trip to the altar, for her husband treated her shamefully. He would go ashore "Where his Wife lived, with whom after he had lain all night, it was his Custom to invite four or five of his brutal Companions to come ashore, and he would force her to prostitute herself to them all, one after another before his Face."

Dissipation and merrymaking marked Blackbeard's life ashore. He entertained on a lavish scale. He courted the friendship of neighboring planters by bestowing gifts of rum and sugar on them. But not even a pirate's fortune could stand up under such a grand scale of living. As his fortune thinned, so did his disposition. He grew sullen. Neighbors who but a short time earlier had been guests in his home now had their own houses plundered. Some were angered by the scandalous fashion in which his crew conducted themselves among the local women, including the wives and daughters of leading citizens. Trading sloops, coming into the North Carolina rivers, were subjected to "insulting & abusing" as Teach plundered them of the goods and liquors that suited his fancy. And so that his activities might not be termed piracy, he always gave his victims a token payment—but never more than a token. Yet so feared was this man that no one dared identify him as the one from whose hands they had received such wretched treatment.

Soon the *Adventure* was being fitted out once again for sea. It was said to be going on a trading voyage to the island of St. Thomas, although the sloop sailed in ballast without a cargo. On board was a crew of twenty men. A few weeks later, Teach once again dropped anchor at Bath in company with a large French merchantman, richly laden with a cargo of sugar, spices, and other merchandise. He had actually taken two French ships off Bermuda, one of which was in ballast. Putting the two crews aboard the empty ship, he had released them before returning to the mainland. Three English ships had been taken also, but they were allowed to continue along their way once Teach had robbed them of provisions.

He gave a ridiculous explanation as to the origin of his prize. Teach swore to Governor Eden that the ship had been found drifting at sea with neither crew nor identifying papers aboard. In the subsequent vice admiralty proceedings, Tobias Knight condemned the prize as a wreck and therefore liable for salvage claims. Yet it seems that Knight never saw the ship, for it had been taken through Ocracoke Inlet and anchored in Pamlico Sound. No one was allowed aboard the prize other than a surgeon to dress the wounds of two men who, it was claimed, were injured by the accidental bursting of a gun. Much of the cargo was taken ashore and stored in a tent.

There was the possibility of future embarrassment should the French institute a search for the ship and identify her as the one taken by pirates. Blackbeard suggested that the prize be destroyed, and Knight prepared a warrant stating that the ship was leaking badly and in danger of sinking and blocking the channel. Eden signed the document and the ship was towed into an inlet not too far from Bath and set on fire. When she had burned to the waterline, the hull was sunk to further conceal all evidence. For their troubles, Governor Eden received sixty hogshead of sugar and Knight twenty.

By this time in Virginia the "Trading People" and other honest citizens, already angered by the pirates' "insolent behavior," were viewing the scene with growing concern. They appealed to Governor Spotswood for aid in removing this canker in their midst. Their uneasiness was given additional weight by the disturbing rumors that Teach planned to fortify an area around Ocracoke as a general rendezvous for pirates, with himself as lord and mentor over them.

More ex-members of Blackbeard's crew were beginning to wander through Virginia. Although they had proof that they had subscribed to the Act of Grace, the governor attempted to disarm as many as possible lest they attempt to capture a ship and "betake themselves again to their old Trade. . . ." Still, there was no real evidence against Teach, and it was suspected that little could be gathered so long as he received the protection of Eden and Knight. Since the pirates supposedly had accepted the King's pardon, any interference on the part of Spotswood would be regarded as usurpation of authority and an official insult. Any effort to accumulate evidence against the pirate had to be carried out in a clandestine manner. About the middle of the summer, Captain Brand of the *Lyme* had sent a man into North Carolina to investigate Blackbeard's activities and to determine if he was living up to the provisions of the Act of Grace.

The first reliable information arose out of the activities of one William Howard, formerly Teach's quartermaster. Howard came into Virginia, bringing with him two Negro boys, one of whom had been taken from a French ship, the other from a ship of English registry. He called attention to himself through the "disorderly manner" in which he lived, and when he began to gather a circle of sailors about him there was reason to suspect that Howard was going "on the account." After his arrest by Captain George Gordon on September 16, 1718, he was kept a prisoner aboard the *Pearl*. There was some question as to the jurisdiction of the Virginia courts should he be brought to trial, but this was clarified when it was discovered that on September 29, 1717, he had participated in the taking of the *Betty* of Virginia and, after plundering her of a number of pipes of Madeira wine, had sunk the sloop. Other charges involved the captures of the *Robert* of Philadelphia, the *Good Intent* of Dublin, and the French ship *Concorde* of St. Malo.

William Howard was not one to submit quietly to what other men considered orderly legal procedures. His insolence bordered on the intolerable, and when it became obvious that he had no visible means of support, one of the local justices of the peace signed a warrant sending Howard aboard the *Pearl* as a vagrant where he was to serve as a regular member of the crew. Howard immediately swore out warrants against the arresting officers—Captain Gordon and Lieutenant Robert Maynard—and the justice who had signed the warrant, charging them with "false impres-

sion" and demanding £500 from each for their libel. The officers had to
post bond in order to continue routine duties. Howard's lawyer was John
Holloway, destined to become the first mayor of Williamsburg and at this
time serving as a judge of the local vice admiralty court. The captains of
the guard ships, harassed and threatened with court action, had attempted
to engage Holloway as their attorney, but discovered that Howard had
already employed him, giving him three ounces of gold as a retainer.

Further investigation brought additional irregularities to light. Richard
Fitzwilliam, collector of customs for the lower James River, was found to
be an "Agent and Solicitor for the Pirates in these parts." He too had been
rewarded by Howard with three ounces of gold dust. As a result of
Howard's strenuous resistance, his past was investigated closely, and it
was then that conclusive evidence was discovered proving him to have
been Teach's quartermaster.

Although Howard protested that he had subscribed to the Act of Grace
and was entitled to its benefits, Spotswood was determined to bring him
to trial on the grounds that he had participated in the taking of no less
than twelve ships after the January 5, 1718, deadline. Even then, there was
some difficulty in persuading the Council that charges should be brought
against Howard. Some of the Council members, apparently friends of
Holloway and Fitzwilliam, based their objections on legal technicalities.
But in the eventual trial Howard was made to appear as "One of the Most
Mischevious and Vilest Villains that had infested that coast," and after
conviction, was sentenced to hang. He escaped the gallows by the oppor-
tune arrival, the night before his execution, of a ship bearing an extension
of the King's mercy to all piracies committed before August 18, 1718.
Howard, advised of the opportunity by the governor's political enemies,
was allowed to take advantage of this extension, but once again was sent
aboard the *Lyme* as an ordinary seaman where, it seems, he performed his
duties without further complaint.

During one session of the General Court, Holloway was soundly
denounced by Spotswood for his activities on behalf of pirates. Both
Brand and Gordon refused to sit on vice admiralty courts with the
attorney. Annoyed, Holloway shouted that never again would he sit as a
judge, an assertion welcomed by the governor, who observed, "I confess

that I was not much displeased at [this] since it gave me an opportunity of putting an honester man in his place."

The evidence presented at Howard's trial clearly established that Blackbeard and his crew had not lived up to the provisions of the Act of Grace, but "like Dogs to their Vomits they have returned to their old detestable way of living. . . ." The pirate was still being watched. In August Captain Brand had sent a second man into Carolina seeking information, and by October word arrived that Teach had brought the French "wreck" into port. There were an increasing number of complaints of the "Insolence of that Gang of Pyrates," and the refusal of the local government to lay restraints on them.

The proximity of so active a group of pirates presented a definite threat to the trade of Virginia, and Spotswood felt it high time that this "Prince of Villains" be eliminated. Still another messenger was dispatched to North Carolina to gain information of the habits and operating methods of Teach, and to escort back to Virginia two Carolina pilots familiar with the shallow waters of the sounds in which the pirates hid.

In carrying through his determination to "Extirpate this Nest of Pyrates," Spotswood conferred with the captains of the two guard ships. They were quick to point out that their heavy men-of-war could not navigate the shallow waters of the Carolina sounds, nor could they maneuver through the difficult winding channels of tributary waters should the pirates choose such an escape route. When the question of hiring small sloops was raised, both Brand and Gordon protested that they were allowed no government funds for such an expedient, and they had no personal funds to be so employed. Both captains did, however, promise the governor that if he could acquire the sloops, they would supply a majority of the men necessary to man them.

Spotswood chartered two sloops with money from his own pocket. There is a suggestion that some of the ex-pirates who had taken the Act of Grace made up a portion of the crew, along with fifty-five seamen from aboard the *Pearl* and the *Lyme*. The larger of the two sloops, given no name in the official dispatches, was placed under the command of Robert Maynard, first lieutenant aboard the *Pearl*. This officer, despite his comparatively low rank, was no youngster; Captain Gordon had earlier referred to Maynard as the oldest lieutenant "in all these foreign parts of America." The smaller sloop, the *Ranger,* was commanded by Midshipman Baker of the *Lyme.* Thirty-five men were aboard the larger vessel, while only twenty-five men made up the crew of the *Ranger.* Captain Ellis Brand was placed in command of the overall expedition. Captain George Gordon was to remain behind with the two frigates, for there was always the possibility that pirates might slip into the bay and create havoc while the crews were understrength.

The two sloops sailed around three o'clock on the afternoon of November 17, 1718. That same night Captain Brand started overland for Bath, there to place Teach under arrest should the pirate be found on shore. Spotswood had already persuaded the Assembly to post a £200 reward for bringing Teach to justice, and for every other pirate captain taken, a payment of £40. For lesser pirates there were varying amounts, down to ordinary seamen, each of whom was worth £10 to his captors. The governor, however, did not inform the Assembly of the purpose of the present expedition for fear that Teach would be informed, "& more especially among the present Faction an unaccountable Inclination to favour Pyrates."

Around two or three o'clock in the afternoon of November 20, entering the narrows of the Roanoke, Maynard spoke with a sloop whose master reported that he had seen Teach's *Adventure* aground on Brant's shoals, with another sloop attempting to get him off. After searching the length of the shoals and finding nothing, Maynard looked into Ocracoke Inlet late in the afternoon of November 21. Two sloops were lying at anchor. Dusk was falling by the time Maynard's vessels worked their way through the inlet. They dropped anchor for the night.

Their appearance came as no great surprise to Teach. A letter from Tobias Knight had warned that the governor of Virginia was exhibiting an unhealthy curiosity and might send out an expedition. Blackbeard cared little and wore no fear. Unlike Maynard, who spent most of the night preparing his sloops for battle, the pirate captain amused himself with drinking and carousing with the master of a merchant sloop that lay anchored not far away. It was during this time that one of his men, in view of the upcoming engagement, asked Teach, should something happen to him, if his wife knew where he had buried his money. The answer was "That no Body but himself and the Devil knew where it was, and the longest Liver should take all."

Maynard began offensive operations about nine o'clock the following morning. Small boats were put over the side to sound the depth of the water between him and the enemy. He needed at least a fathom beneath his keel in which to maneuver if he was to outwit the more heavily armed pirate. As the small boats wandered within range of the *Adventure,* a round of shot sent them hastily pulling back to their own vessels. Maynard ordered the *Ranger,* because of her shallow draft, to move in and board the pirate. His sloop would follow. Maynard's ship ran aground, but was refloated when her ballast was thrown over the side. A few moments later the *Ranger* was stuck fast on a sand bar. She was lightened by emptying the water casks. Maynard maneuvered in towards the pirate. According to one source, the following conversation was shouted across the water.

Teach, standing on deck, hailed Maynard with, "Damn you for Villains, Who are you? And, from whence came you?"

Maynard, running up the British ensign, replied, "You can see by our Colours that we are no Pyrates."

Teach bellowed an invitation to come aboard so that he might see who they were.

Maynard, still fighting the battle of words, indicated his intention of boarding the *Adventure* with, "I cannot spare my Boat, but I will come aboard of you as soon as I can with my Sloop."

Swilling a long dram from his mug of rum, Teach leaped to the top of the round house and cried, "Damnation seize my Soul if I give you Quarters or take any from you."

Maynard closed the debate with the reply, "That he expected no Quarters from him, nor should he give him any."

With this Teach ran up his "black Ensign with the Death's Head." Anchor cables were cut as sails were unfurled. He made for the channel that Maynard had entered by. Midshipman Baker, following Maynard's orders, threw over the helm of the *Ranger* so as to block the pirate's passage to the open sea. When, within "half a pistol shot," the *Adventure* swung around and delivered a broadside, Midshipman Baker and his second and third in command were killed, along with several seamen. Thomas Tucker, master mate, assumed command of the stricken vessel, but with her jib and foremast shot away, the *Ranger* began to drift helplessly and was all but out of the fight.

The breeze died. Maynard broke out his sweeps and began to pull towards the *Adventure*. The *Ranger,* still within range though drifting, kept up a desultory fire. Blackbeard hove to as his fore halliards and jib sheet were shot away. As Maynard's sloop crept into range, Teach, noting that its crew were crowded on deck manning the sweeps, primed his guns with swan, partridge, and other small shot. His broadside swept clean the deck of Maynard's sloop as twenty-one men fell wounded.

Maynard, fearful of a slaughter, ordered his men below decks and he himself retired to the safety of his cabin. On deck was a midshipman and a Mr. Butler, the pilot who had been brought from North Carolina. These two lonely men shouted down information to Maynard as the situation developed. The sloop scraped bottom, but was quickly worked off into deep water.

Teach, seeing the empty deck of his adversary, assured himself that there were no longer enough men on board to offer effective resistance. He set a course for Maynard's vessel. The *Adventure* was brought alongside. Handmade grenades, bottles filled with powder, small shot and scrap iron, with fuses smoking, were tossed onto the deck of Maynard's sloop. The explosions did little damage. Through the smoke, a few of Maynard's men could be spotted running about the deck. Blackbeard encouraged his men with the cry "That they were all knock'd on the Head, except three or four, and therefore Let's jump on Board, and cut them to Pieces." The pirate captain was the first to board, rope in hand to lash the two sloops together.

As the pirates scrambled over the gunwales, Butler gave the word to Maynard who ordered his men up on deck and he "himself was presently among them." Amidst angry shouts, crackling pistol shots, and the clatter of swinging cutlasses, Blackbeard and Maynard met face to face. Both fired pistols at almost point blank range. Teach missed. Maynard's ball plowed into the massive body facing him. The pirate barely wavered and

The fight between Lieutenant Maynard and Blackbeard which resulted in the death of the infamous Teach.

drove forward, his heavy cutlass swinging. A powerful sweep of Blackbeard's weapon snapped Maynard's cutlass like a twig. As he drew back his mighty arm to deliver the death blow, one of Maynard's men reached out and slashed Teach's throat. The glancing blow by the pirate caught Maynard across the knuckles. Even after he became a prime target for his enemies, Blackbeard fought on. He jerked another pistol from his belt. While in the act of cocking the firearm, he suddenly toppled over dead. Twenty-five wounds, five of which had been inflicted by pistol balls, had finally sapped the life from his magnificent body. He had found dying more difficult than living.

It had been a short engagement; some said that it lasted less than ten minutes. With at least nine of the *Adventure's* crew sprawled lifeless near the body of their captain, several others leaped overboard where "they were demolished." The remainder threw down their arms and begged for mercy.

Down in the hold of the *Adventure,* another struggle had been taking place. One of the pirate crew, a Negro by the name of Caesar, had been stationed beside a train of powder leading to the magazine. His orders, should Maynard's men gain the victory, were to blow up the ship. A planter who had been forced aboard the *Adventure* the night before and held prisoner in the hold during the fight, overpowered Caesar and forced him away from the powder train.

All nine pirate survivors, three white men and six Negroes, had been wounded. Of Maynard's men, ten had been killed, while another twenty-five had been wounded, one of whom later died. One had been shot through the body by one of his own shipmates in the mistaken idea that he was a pirate. A search of Teach's belongings brought to light several interesting documents. There were several letters from prominent New York merchants. Another beginning "My Friend," and signed "T. Knight," contained a veiled warning and suggested that Governor Eden would welcome an early visit from the pirate. An account book recorded the disposition of the booty taken, while a memorandum confirmed Knight's implication with the pirates. Shortly afterwards, Blackbeard's head was severed from his body and the grisly trophy swung beneath the bowsprit of Maynard's sloop.

In the meantime, Captain Brand had traveled overland as a "Single Gentleman," accompanied by a servant. Near Bath he met with Maurice Moore, Edward Moseley, and others who had grown "weary of that rogues insolence." Colonel Moore slipped into town to see if Teach was there. He returned to say that the pirate was not around, but was expected at almost any moment. Brand continued on into town and, presenting himself to Governor Eden, informed him of his mission.

Two days passed. There was no news of Maynard. Brand sent out men in two canoes in search of information. Two more days passed before they returned with the news that Blackbeard had been killed and that Lieutenant Maynard had already taken aboard 140 sacks of cocoa and ten casks of sugar from the tent at Ocracoke. Brand ordered Maynard to sail up to Bath. During this interval, Knight was advising Eden against cooperation with the naval officer and constantly presented arguments justifying Teach's actions while in North Carolina. Undeterred, Brand demanded, and with the governor's seeming cooperation, confiscated sixty hogsheads and twenty barrels of sugar, along with six Negroes that no one seemed to want to claim and were now declared pirate plunder. Some of the sugar and some cotton goods were discovered hidden in a barn owned by Tobias Knight, although that worthy swore that he had nothing to do with pirates. Six members of Blackbeard's crew, including Israel Hands, were found to be in Bath and all were taken prisoners. Everything was loaded aboard the two sloops and sent to Williamsburg, Blackbeard's head still swinging beneath the bowsprit of Maynard's sloop.

Maynard's orders from Brand had been that all goods taken from the pirates be placed in the hold and the hatches sealed until their disposition could be determined by a court of vice admiralty. This was to include the gold, plate, and other goods found aboard the *Adventure*. Brand had started his journey back to Williamsburg shortly after issuing these orders. Against the express instructions of the captain, Maynard shared out the items taken from the pirate sloop, retaining for himself three-eighths as due a captain and commander.

This disobedience of direct orders by Maynard became but one of the many controversies arising out of the Blackbeard affair. Governor Eden now had second thoughts about his cooperation with Captain Brand. He challenged the legality of the entire operation, charging that Spotswood had exceeded his authority in dispatching the sloops into North Carolina. The pirates who had submitted to the Act of Grace, he declared, were under his protection and if they were to be tried, that trial should be held in North Carolina, for they were residents of that colony. Even if both governors could claim equal authority, Eden should have jurisdiction over the disposition of the pirate goods, "for where two people have equal rights, he that hath the possession ought to have the performance."

Those goods allegedly belonging to the pirates, said attorney Thomas Pollock, should not have been taken out of the colony without the express permission of the Lords Proprietors or the King. If, as Spotswood claimed, he planned to try the pirates under the commission formerly granted Francis Nicholson as governor, that commission expired when Nicholson was replaced. Although Pollock thought that "There seems to be a great deal of malice and design in their management of this affair," he went on to suggest to Eden that "as for the trial of the men, if they have it in Virginia, it [will] ease your Honour of a great deal of trouble and take off the odium of it from this Government." In retrospect, it appears that the loss of the sugar and other goods prompted Eden's protest; seven weeks earlier no such arguments about jurisdiction had been lodged with Governor Johnson when Stede Bonnet was taken by South Carolina sloops in the Cape Fear.

Spotswood worried little about the protests and was determined that the captured pirates be made an example of. As justification of his actions, he pointed out that Blackbeard and his crew had taken the French ship after they had accepted the Act of Grace. Of this he could be sure, for the crippled Israel Hands had agreed to turn King's evidence.

Much of the evidence implicating Tobias Knight with Teach was supplied by Hands. Maurice Moore, Edward Moseley, and Jeremiah Vail of North Carolina, whose complaints were indirectly responsible for the capture of the pirates, undertook to supply additional evidence. They submitted a request to examine the records of the colony. This was promptly denied. On December 27, 1718, they entered by force the house of John Lovick, deputy-secretary of the colony. Nailing shut all doors and windows of the room in which the records were stored, they spent the next twenty-four hours shuffling papers in their search for evidence to be used against Knight. Governor Eden, righteously deploring this "unlawful and improper action," dispatched a large possee to arrest them, leading Moseley to make the bitter observation that "the Governor could find men enough to arrest peacable citizens, but none to arrest thieves and robbers."

Still, Eden could not afford to ignore the charges building up against Tobias Knight, especially after Spotswood sent him a copy of the testimony of Israel Hands and demanded that the secretary be sent to England for trial. On May 27, 1719, Knight defended himself before the Governor's Council. The letter found in Teach's effects was compared with other documents and found to be in Knight's hand. Despite this damaging evidence, the Council, rallying to the support of the governor and his secretary, saw Knight as a "good and faithful Officer," and the evidence against him they found to be "false and malitious," and he was cleared of all charges of conspiracies with pirates.

Moseley and Moore, who had labored so hard to clean up the situation in North Carolina, did not get off so easily. They were brought before the General Court, dominated by members of the Council. Both were found guilty. Moore received a fine of only £5, but Moseley, who had been more openly critical of Governor Eden's lack of action against the pirates, was made an example of. He was not convicted of breaking into Lovick's house, however. For speaking "false malitious scandalous Opprebious & seditious words" against the governor, not only was he fined £100, but he was forbidden to hold any public office for the next three years.

The surviving members of Teach's crew had also been brought to trial. On the grounds that they had taken the French ship off the Bermudas on August 22, they were not eligible for the King's extension of the Act of Grace. All but one were convicted and sentenced to be hanged. Samuel Odell, who had received over seventy wounds in the fight with Maynard's men, was able to prove that he had been forced from a merchant vessel just the night before the engagement and was acquitted. Thirteen met their death beneath the gallows. Although Israel Hands was found guilty and received the death sentence, he was allowed to claim the extension of the Act of Grace as a reward for his evidence, and it was assumed that he had not taken part in the taking of the French prize. He returned to England and for years limped about the streets of London, a whining beggar.

Greed kept the controversy alive. Everyone seemed to want a share of the captured pirate treasure, leading Spotswood to observe, "People are easily led to favor these Pests of Mankind when they have hopes of Sharing in their ill-gotten Wealth." Among those who claimed a share were the Lords Proprietors of Carolina, who resorted to subtle blackmail by suggesting to Spotswood that they would not question the legality of his actions if they received the share they felt was rightfully theirs. Their interest may well have been the reason for Eden's change of heart, for he had been more than cooperative with Captain Brand, and on the return trip had even ridden as far as the next county with the naval captain.

When the pirate goods were being considered for condemnation by the vice admiralty court, a lawyer from North Carolina appeared before that body, contesting the jurisdiction of the court and arguing that Brand had taken the pirate goods by force. Inasmuch as the goods had been taken in North Carolina, he declared that the Lords Proprietors were entitled to their proper shares, or the goods should be returned to North Carolina for proper admiralty adjudication. His arguments proved weak and the Virginia court condemned the plunder and ordered that it be sold. Perhaps both Eden and the Proprietors should have quietly ignored the entire affair, for within a year there was the charge and recommendation that because of "their entertaining Pirates they are justly contemmed by their neighbours, for which reason and that they may be under good Government and be made usefull to the rest of His Majesty's Collonys it would be proper to joyn the same again to Virginia."

The pirate goods were sold at public auction for the sum of £2,247 19s. 7d., Virginia currency, a sum not representing their true worth. There was also the reward of £280 allowed by the Virginia Assembly for the capture of Blackbeard's crew. No reward was allowed for the pirate captain and those of his crew who had been killed, for they had not been taken alive and brought to justice as stated in Spotswood's proclamation announcing the reward. This reward money, to be distributed among the crew, likewise became a source of contention. One twelfth was allotted to the civilian crew of the sloops Spotswood had employed, for they had made up that percentage of the crews that had taken the pirates. Brand and Gordon received £334 13s. 6d. to be divided between the crews of the *Pearl* and the *Lyme* who, although they did not actually participate in the capture, had stayed behind and performed their duties and were entitled to share under customary naval practice. Brand and Gordon turned over their personal shares to Maynard's men, each of whom received £1 13s. 6d. Those who remained behind shared out at 9s. 6d. each. For his leadership, Maynard was allowed two shares.

Despite the generosity of Captains Gordon and Brand, Maynard and Tucker protested that they had been mistreated and, in communications to the admiralty, charged both captains with withholding shares from the men. In their defense, the captains submitted reports presenting evidence that Maynard had not been the fearless leader that he had pictured himself in his own account. In addition to this irritation, both naval captains were harassed by Robert Fitzwilliam because of the embarrassments they had caused him in the past; he charged them exorbitant custom duties on items they declared personal property. Eventually, because of the complaints lodged by Maynard and the Proprietors of Carolina, Gordon and Brand were recalled to England and suspended from duty until the controversies were settled.

Some of the men who had fought the pirates later went out on the account for themselves. Lieutenant Maynard may have resigned or retired from the Royal Navy and perhaps settled down in Prince George County. The records indicate that a Captain Maynard was murdered in that area by two Negro slaves in the late 1720's.

Spotswood also suffered for his zeal in the suppression of piracy. His political enemies, along with "malicious Whisperers, Clandestine Informers, and Anonymous Libellers of Government" (as he characterized them), declared that: "As to the destroying of Thache and his Crew that Story had better be kept in silence than told for if all the Circumstances of it were known they would make little for his reputation." Others charged that the governor demanded a fee from every pirate to whom he extended the Act of Grace. Other rumors implied that Blackbeard and his crew had been entitled to the benefits of the King's proclamation, but had been denied its benefits by Spotswood. In North Carolina an effort was made to prove that the pirates had committed no piratical acts since they had received the Act of Grace. The House of Burgesses appeared so reluctant to appropriate funds to pay certain expenses incurred in the capture of the pirates that Spotswood vowed that he would pay them out of his own pocket. On the other hand, Spotswood received addresses of appreciation from the merchants and masters of trading vessels operating out of North Carolina, the governor and Council of Maryland, and the College of William and Mary.

The successful capture had revealed some strange bedfellows in Virginia. And the name of Blackbeard was destined to loom larger in history and romance than that of the man who engineered his destruction.

VII

LADY PIRATES AND
BLOODTHIRSTY MEN

"My Lord, we plead our bellies."

Twenty-five years of intense and near continuous piracy had been almost too much for the American colonies to bear. In those communities where pirates had been looked on with some favor, opinion hardened against them as the benefits of trade with these outlaws of the sea were overbalanced by their depredations. So great had grown the aggravations that proper caution was not always exercised when suspected pirates fell into the hands of the authorities. In Virginia there was one incident in which, unjustly, three men were almost executed. If no one believed their stories, it was surely because they pleaded the same defense as did most accused pirates.

In late 1718, Henry Mann, William Stoke, and Aure Van Pelt were brought before the Virginia court, charged with taking the *Providence* off the coast of South Carolina. In presenting their defense, they admitted that they had formerly been members of Charles Vane's crew; but they declared that they, along with a number of their shipmates, had resolved to desert the company and take advantage of the King's proclamation. This group had been placed aboard a prize that Vane had taken, whose principal cargo had been ninety Negroes. They, in turn, had sighted and chased the sloop *Providence,* primarily because they needed a pilot to guide them across the treacherous bar at Charleston. They had planned to take the prize into that port and submit to the local authorities. Once the

Providence was taken, these three men had been placed aboard the sloop as something of a prize crew. Their story seemed thin; they were sentenced to be hanged.

Before the sentence could be carried out, it was learned that these pirates had indeed planned to go into Charleston. The remainder of the crew aboard the slave ship had managed to cross the Charleston bar, surrendering the ninety slaves to the authorities and throwing themselves on the King's mercy. Adverse winds, it was learned, had blown the *Providence* far enough off course that they had veered within the jurisdiction of the Virginia courts. Once their good intentions had been verified, it was decided that they were "fit objects of his Majesties mercy." Yet, on the other hand, it was felt that, as vagrants, they should not "be allowed the Liberty of Stragling about the Country; being persons of whose behaviour the Government can have but Small Confidence." They were given the usual sentence for stray seamen—service in the crew of the guard ship stationed in Virginia.

Governor Johnson of South Carolina was as active in his drive against pirates as was Alexander Spotswood of Virginia. A certain pirate captain by the name of Richard Worley had of late made a nuisance of himself off the coasts of Virginia and the Carolinas. Worley was relatively inexperienced in the pirate business. In September, 1718, he, along with eight companions, had sailed out of New York in a small open boat, their only supplies a few ship biscuits, a couple of dried tongues, "a little Cag of Water," half-a-dozen old muskets, and ammunition. Not until they reached the Delaware River did they capture a sloop that fitted their designs. Once fitted out in proper pirate fashion, they cruised the coast and the Bahamas, taking a number of prizes.

Two months later, in a brigantine, the *Eagle,* and a sloop, the *New York Revenge's Revenge,* they lay off Charleston harbor. Several prizes were taken, even as Stede Bonnet languished in his prison. Because Governor Johnson had refused to honor his promise of intercession for mercy to Bonnet, William Rhett refused to have anything to do with any attempt to eliminate this new pirate threat. Johnson pressed four ships into service, the *Mediterranean,* the *King William,* the *Sea Nymph* and Bonnet's *Royal James,* a little fleet mounting some seventy guns. Johnson personally assumed command of the expedition, and several members of the Council, along with "other Gentlemen of the Country," were included among the 300 volunteers.

During the early morning hours of November 5, 1718, they slipped out of Charleston harbor. Worley, believing them to be merchantmen, stood in towards the harbor mouth to intercept them. As the pirate ran up his black flag with a demand to surrender, Johnson answered him with a broadside. As Worley's ships bore away, Johnson attempted to hem them in between his vessels and the shore. The *Eagle* managed to escape to the open sea. The *Sea Nymph* and the *Royal James* fought the *New York Revenge's Revenge* yardarm to yardarm for the next four hours before Worley was killed and the remainder of his crew surrendered. Johnson pursued the *Eagle* until four that afternoon when, after one broadside, the crew of the brigantine lowered their flag. In addition to Worley, twenty-six other pirates had been killed. Nineteen pirates were brought ashore and hanged. Five were acquitted. With Bonnet's crew, this meant a total of forty-nine pirates hanged in South Carolina in one month's time. Aboard Worley's ships there had been 106 convicts, including thirty-six women, who had been transported out of England to be sold as indentured servants in Virginia or Maryland. They were sold on the Charleston market, with one-half of the proceeds going to the owners of the sloops used in the capture of the pirates, the other half shared among the captors.

The elimination of Bonnet, Teach, Worley, and other pirates did little to assuage the general situation, but it was a beginning. William Byrd observed in 1719 that "These Rogues swarm in this part of the World," and was told that there were at least seventy pirate crews active off the coast of North America. Perhaps the greatest change was that the pirates now seem to have declared war on honest men and seemed bent on revenge for those colleagues who had fallen victims to the forces of law and order. Now, their treatment of prisoners bordered on the homicidal.

Constant problems arose out of piratical activities in far off seas. One such incident came about as a result of the capture of the *West River*, a merchantman out of London bound for Virginia. She was taken by the *Rover*, whose captain used the name of "Callifax," but was in reality one Thomas Kennedy, who had but recently deserted the company of Captain Bartholomew Roberts. Luke Knott, the Quaker captain of the *West River*, and his crew were held captive for nine days while the pirates plundered his ship. Eight pirates had obtained permission to resign from the company, and Knott was given his ship and allowed to continue his voyage on the condition that he would land them in Virginia. Once on the mainland, they planned to disperse themselves in Maryland and North Carolina, living as people of the country. Their share of the plunder was three Negro men and a boy, some coin and gold dust, in all amounting to about £800 in value. For his troubles, and in return for his silence, Knott was presented with ten chests of tea, ten rolls of tobacco, gold dust, and a number of Portuguese gold moidores. Gold was likewise distributed among his crew.

Once inside the Virginia capes, four of the pirates parted company with the *West River,* sailing for Maryland in a small shallop they had brought along with them. The remaining four, who intended traveling overland to North Carolina, continued with Knott as he turned into the James River. At his first opportunity Captain Knott informed Governor Spotswood of the character of his passengers. They were seized. Their four companions encountered a sudden squall in the bay and were forced back into the York River, where they met with "good Entertainment among the Planters." Once their whereabouts was known, Thomas Wythe and four companions captured the four pirates.

Tried before the vice admiralty court in February, 1720, six of the pirates, "the most profligate Wretches I ever heard of," demonstrated their contempt for the bench by conducting themselves with the "greatest Impudence at the Bar." No sooner had they been convicted than they roundly cursed the judges and everyone else concerned with the court, and loudly vowed they would give no quarter to those who fell into their hands in the future, but would murder them on sight.

Because of their arrogance, Spotswood thought it necessary for the "greater Terrour" to hang four of them in chains, two at Tindall's Point on the York River, two at Urbanna on the Rappahannock. The other two were hanged without that indignity being visited upon them. Two others, "who shew'd a just Abhorrence of their past Crimes," Spotswood sent aboard the local guard ship as ordinary seamen. As in all cases where pirate gold was involved, complications continued. Before they had been captured by Wythe, the four pirates originally bound for Maryland had managed to cache a considerable amount of gold with the local planters. There was an intensive search before it could all be brought together.

Captain Knott not only forced his men to give up the gold given them in return for their silence, but he likewise surrendered the presents that had been bestowed on him. Subsequent events proved that his honesty did not pay. Because of his forthrightness, Knott was forced to give up his seafaring career, "on Account of the Pirates threatening to Torture him to Death if he ever falls into their hands."

Equally perplexing was the case of Captain Thomas Kennedey of the *Calibar* of Bristol. In March, 1720, Kennedey came into Virginia with a strange tale. Off the Guinea coast his ship had been taken by Captain Edward England. Kennedey's crew had been abused and beaten and the entire group kept as prisoners for nine months. Not only was his cargo of trade goods, copper bars, beads, guns, and powder looted, but some of the 160 slaves aboard, claimed by the pirates, died as a result of the casual treatment given them by their new masters. Even then, Kennedey and his men came off well, for England had a habit of mistreating his prisoners

Kennedey's crew throws broken glass at a prisoner.

by beating them with his cutlass and nicking them about the ears. On one occasion he had allowed his men to lash a captured captain to a windlass, pelt him with broken glass until he was cut "in a sad Manner." Then, streaming blood, the victim was whipped about the deck until "at last, because he had been a good Master to his Men, they said, he should have an easy Death, and so shot him thro' the Head."

England and his company took a fancy to Kennedey. When he and his crew were eventually allowed to continue their voyage to Virginia, the captain was given a present of twenty-one Negroes, two iron guns, and a small hawser, "as a Satisfaction for the Damage they had done him." They had taken some English coin from him, but in return they had bestowed on him Portuguese moidores of greater value.

On his arrival in Virginia, Kennedey turned over not only the Negroes, but the coin to Spotswood, who accepted them for the Crown on the ground that pirates could not legally transfer property. He did, however, allow £126 for the Negroes, thereby setting off a lengthy legal dispute with the owners of the *Calibar*. They argued that this amount was only about one-fourth the true value of the Negroes, and petitioned that they be granted £1200 for damages to their vessel and cargo or else the Negroes be turned over to them. Eventually, they were given the Negroes.

The suppression of piracy had now become something of an obsession with Governor Spotswood. His efforts were strengthened somewhat by the passage of a new piracy act in 1720 which added to the scope of piracy, stating that all those who "shall trade with, by truck, barter, or exchange, with any pirate. . . . if found guilty such persons will be esteemed pirates." The governor was quick to apply this statute, bringing before the court one Joseph Stretton, late master of the *Prince Eugene* of Bristol. When it was determined that Stretton had indeed traded with the pirates of Madagascar, he was ordered to England for trial as an accessory to piracy.

The greatest danger to shipping in the fall of 1721 was the host of Spanish privateers that harassed the Virginia coast. Although Spain and England were not formally at war, St. Augustine in Florida had become a "Resort of Banditty," and the governor of that colony issued commissions that did not conform to any general pattern. One Nicholas de Conception, a Spanish mulatto, discovered that the Virginia guard ship was careened, and swept through the capes to take several prizes almost within sight of land. One was retaken by the lieutenant of the guard ship who commandeered a sloop and gave pursuit. This issue was eased somewhat after Spotswood dispatched a flag of truce to St. Augustine. The governor there released several of the prizes, but refused to give up those with more valuable cargoes, claiming that they were smugglers and therefore legitimate prizes.

Still more unsettling was an impudent message from the pirate Bartholomew Roberts, referred to as the "Great Pirate Roberts." He had cruised the coasts of both North and South America. So formidable had his reputation grown that the guard ships stationed in the West Indies were reluctant to tangle with him, and indeed, seemed to sail out of their way to avoid a confrontation. Roberts was a tall man, of dark complexion and "good natural Parts, and personal Bravery, tho' he applied them to such wicked Purposes. . . ." He was also a dandy among pirates, dressing himself in rich crimson damask waistcoat and breeches, a red feather in his hat, and a diamond cross suspended at the end of the gold chain around his neck. In action, in addition to his sword, he wore two pairs of pistols at the end of the silk sling across his shoulder.

Roberts's natural boldness was more effective because of his reliance on the unusual. Toward the end of June, 1720, he had sailed a sloop of ten guns, manned by sixty men, into Trepassey in Newfoundland. Sailing into the harbor, "with their black Colours flying, Drums beating, and Trumpets sounding," he was both a surprising and awesome sight. The crews of the twenty-two ships lying at anchor immediately quitted their vessels and fled to the safety of the shore. Roberts wreaked havoc among the shipping, sinking all but one brigantine he needed to transport his booty. In the open seas outside the harbor he met up with a sizeable French flotilla which he destroyed except for one large brigantine that he made his flagship, renaming her the *Royal Fortune*. The brigantine they had taken from Trepassey was now loaded with French prisoners, "for they would not force or permit any of any nation to be with them only English."

Roberts created an uproar in Virginia in the spring of 1721, when a sloop he had captured and released off Bermuda came in with a message from this arch-pirate. Roberts sent word that just as soon as he was joined

The flag of the "Great Pirate Roberts."

by another pirate ship, they would come in to visit the colony, seeking revenge for those pirates who had been executed there. And in inflicting their vengeance, they promised "they would not spare man woman or Child found in the Country."

Bartholomew Roberts was capable of such enmity. He bore the people of the islands of Martinique and Barbados such hatred that his black flag bore an image of himself, one hand grasping a flaming sword, each foot resting on a human skull. Beneath one skull were the letters A.B.H., meaning "A Barbadian's Head," beneath the other, A.M.H. for "A Martinican's Head." His message to Spotswood became even more ominous with the news that Roberts had captured a French man-of-war with the governor of Martinique on board; the pirates, or so the story ran, had hanged the governor from the yardarm. Others on board had their ears sliced off or were lashed to the yardarm and used for target practice.

The guard ship stationed in Virginia could offer little resistance if Roberts chose to follow through with his threat. His *Royal Fortune* of forty-two guns was accompanied by an eighteen-gun brigantine, the *Sea King*. There were 262 white men and fifty Negroes making up the crews of these two vessels. And, he had said that he would be accompanied by another pirate in a brigantine of sixteen guns. Spotswood persuaded the Council to authorize the construction of batteries mounting a total of sixty guns at the mouths of the James, York, and Rappahannock rivers.

The governor's uneasiness continued after Roberts had been killed at sea, in an engagement off the coast of Africa. Two years after he was replaced as governor of Virginia he was afraid to return to England to give an account of his stewardship because of "the Vigorous part I've acted to Suppress Pirates: and if those barbarous Wretches can be moved to cut off the Nose & Ears of a Master for but correcting his own Sailors, what inhuman Treatment must I expect, should I fall within their power, who have been markt as the principal Object of their Vengeance, for cutting off their arch Pirate Thatch, with all his grand Designs, & making so many of their fraternity to swing in the open air of Virginia."

Yet the North American coast was gradually made safe for shipping as the more notorious pirates were captured and hanged. One of them, the "famous fellow name Vane," had been executed about the same time that Roberts had been threatening the Virginians and may well have been the pirate that Roberts was expecting to join him.

Vane was one of those who had successfully fished the Spanish wrecks off Cape Canaveral, and his name was particularly feared as a pirate. His company had been in that "Colony of Rogues," New Providence, when Woodes Rogers, accompanied by two men-of-war, came in to assume his duties as governor. Vane and his men would have nothing to do with the King's pardon as offered by Rogers, especially after he refused to assure them that if they did submit they would be allowed to retain their accumulated plunder. As soon as the men-of-war entered the harbor, the

Merchantman under attack by Charles Vane.

pirates set fire to a prize they had brought in and, with their black flag flying, sailed out into the open sea, firing an insolent shot at one of the naval vessels as they went off. A short time later Vane sent in a message to Rogers, threatening to come in and burn the local guard ship.

In the spring of 1718 Vane had cruised the shipping lanes off the New England coast. By fall, he was off South Carolina where a number of his men, under one Yeats, slipped away into the North Edisto River to accept the King's pardon, much to the chagrin of their former captain. Vane, or Vaughan, as he was sometimes called, captured a number of prizes outside the Charleston bar.

It was then that Governor Johnson fitted out two sloops and placed them under the command of William Rhett to capture the pirates in the Cape Fear. Vane, learning this, purposely allowed prisoners to overhear conversation to the effect that he was going to careen in one of the rivers to the south. Then, setting them free to spread the word, he set his sails and steered north. Rhett swallowed the bait and searched the rivers and bays to the south before turning back to his original objective, the pirates in the Cape Fear. All of this had been but a prelude to the capture of Stede Bonnet.

Vane had sailed on to a rendevous with his friend, Teach, perhaps to discuss the establishment of a new pirate haven along the North Carolina coast. As Vane beat his way through Ocracoke Inlet, he saluted his friend in the pirate fashion, that is, with his guns fully charged, but aimed wide or angled upward. Teach returned the salute, after which "mutual Civilities passed for some time." Vane sailed northward in early October.

Cruising first off the capes of Virginia, and then in the vicinity of New York, Vane took several vessels. But now his luck was running out. One vessel refused to heave to, and answered his hail with a broadside after the black flag had been run up. The prospective prize ran up her own colors, revealing herself to be a French man-of-war. Vane gave the order to make off. His quartermaster, John Rackham, protested, arguing that they could take on the warship with no danger. Both had support among the crew, but Vane's word carried the day.

The men continued to grumble and argue amongst themselves. The following day, "the Captain's Behaviour was obliged to stand the Test of a Vote, and a Resolution passed against his Honour and Dignity, branding him with the Name of Coward, deposing him from the Command, and turning him out of the Company, with Marks of Infamy; and with him, went all those who did not Vote for boarding the French Man of War." They were placed aboard a small sloop and Vane's former shipmates, with Rackham now elected captain in his stead, sailed away.

Vane and his men sailed about the Caribbean until his sloop was wrecked. Most of his crew were drowned and he was cast away on a small uninhabited island near the Bay of Honduras. Here he lived for some weeks, kept alive by the fishermen who came to that place in search of the great turtles that came ashore. A ship from Jamaica, captained by an ex-pirate and a former friend of Vane's, a Captain Holford, came in to take on water. In reply to Vane's plea that he be taken off, Holford replied, "Charles, I shan't trust you aboard my Ship, unless I carry you a Prisoner; for I shall have you caballing with my Men, knock me on the Head, and run away with my Ship a-pyrating." In answer to Vane's protestations of the most honorable of intentions, Holford told him that, if on his return voyage a month hence, he discovered that he was still on the island, Vane would be carried to Jamaica to be hanged.

Things looked better when Vane persuaded another captain to take him off the island. It so happened that his rescuer was likewise a friend of Holford's, and when the two met at sea, they furled sails to exchange pleasantries. Happening to spot Vane, Holford revealed the pirate's true identity. The rescuer being only too happy to rid himself of Vane, Holford took him aboard and carried him to Jamaica. There he was delivered into the hands of justice to be hanged. It must have been some satisfaction to Vane that Rackham was also brought in about this same time.

John Rackham was a picturesque character, called "Calico Jack" because of the striped material he fancied for his trousers. His fortunes had been checkered after he assumed the command of Vane's ship, although his men stood steady with him during this period. He was too successful in the Caribbean, where his marauding led Woodes Rogers to fit out a sloop under a Captain Burnet to go out and eliminate this menace to shipping. Burnet surprised Rackham while he was entertaining other pirates and brought him into St. Jago de la Vega to be tried, convicted, and hanged in chains. The greatest surprise came when the pirates, after

The lady pirates, Mary Read and Anne Bonny. An engraving from the original edition of Johnson's *A General History of the Pirates,* 1724.

conviction, were brought to the bar to be asked if there was any reason why sentence of death should not be passed upon them. From two there came the astounding answer:

"My Lord, we plead our bellies."

These two lady pirates, Mary Read and Anne Bonny, were pleading pregnancy as a reason for temporarily escaping the hangman's noose.

Mary Read's life was like a strange and wondrous novel, and indeed much of it may have been the fabrication of a romantic soul. Her mother, "who was young and airy," had found herself with child after her husband had been more than a year at sea. To conceal her indiscretion from her husband's kin, Mary's mother dressed the girl in boys' clothing to impersonate her legitimate son whose death she had not reported to the relatives. Mary Read was thus brought up as a boy, a disguise she was to frequent the greater part of her life.

Military and naval life seemed to hold a fascination for the maid. Large for her age, she served as a "Foot-boy" aboard a man-of-war until she became a cadet in a regiment of foot, where "she behaved herself with a great deal of Bravery." But she could not repress basic female instincts when next she enlisted in a regiment of cavalry. Among her messmates was a handsome young fellow with whom she fell in love. Inasmuch as "Mars and Venus could not be served at the same time," her military habits vacillated from exemplary to sloppy. She mooned so constantly that the one she admired thought her mad, until she worked up enough courage to reveal her sex to him. This delighted the young man who was happy that he would have a mistress in the field, but she resisted all advances until he promised to marry her.

After the campaign, Mary Read changed into woman's dress to take the marriage vows. This affair, "Two Troopers marrying each other, made a great noise." The officers of the regiment were so intrigued that they contributed enough money to enable the newlyweds to establish a tavern, the sign of the "Three Horseshoes," near Breda, in Holland where, it is said, it is still standing today. The early death of her husband, the end of the war, and the removal of English military customers from Holland, brought an end to temporary prosperity. Once again the young widow donned male clothing and joined a regiment of foot, at the time on garrison duty in Holland.

It was an interlude of peace, and Mary Read grew restless. Having taken "a Resolution of seeking her Fortune another Way," she left the army and shipped out as a sailor aboard a Dutch vessel bound for the West Indies. Her ship was stopped by pirates, and as she was the only English seaman aboard, they carried Mary with them when the prize was allowed to continue her voyage. There is no record as to the captain of this ship, but when the King's proclamation offering clemency was published, the entire company went in and surrendered themselves.

Her money was soon spent. Hearing that Woodes Rogers was commissioning privateers against the Spanish she went to New Providence. Once aboard a privateer, she joined others of the crew in rising against the captain and going on the account again. Eventually, still disguised as a male, she found herself under the command of Calico Jack Rackham.

Mary Read held herself somewhat aloof from the rest of the company and seems to have been accepted as a man until once again love complicated matters. Rackham had a mistress aboard, also disguised as a man. This Anne Bonny, "who was not altogether so reserved in point of chastity," took Mary Read to be a handsome young pirate and began to make advances, revealing her own sex in the process. This, in turn, forced

Mary to confide that she was also a female in disguise, to the vast disappointment of Anne. Still, they became fast friends, but this intimacy so disturbed Jack Rackham that he threatened to slit the throat of the man he took to be Anne's lover and, as a consequence, was allowed to share the secret.

Anne Bonny had not lived so adventurous a life as Mary Read, but she had lived hard. She was the bastard daughter of an attorney of Cork in Ireland, whose wife left him because of his dissolute way of life. Her mother was a maid in her father's household. At first Anne dressed as a boy, her father pretending that she was the son of friends who had been apprenticed to him to learn the legal business. Later, casting aside all pretensions and living openly with his former maid, the attorney's practice so fell off that he was forced to seek his fortune elsewhere.

Her father, his doxy, and their daughter sailed for Carolina, where he was successful enough as both a lawyer and a merchant to purchase a large plantation. When Anne's mother died, the young girl took over the duties of her father's housekeeper.

She grew up to be a robust lass, and "was of a fierce and coragious Temper." Her disposition was so waspish, it was whispered but never proven, that during one of her fits of passion she had killed a serving girl with a knife. And it was common knowledge that when one young man attempted to force the young vixen against her will, she thrashed him so soundly that he was confined to his bed for several weeks.

Anne was turned out of her father's home when she married James Bonny, a young sailor "not worth a Groat." Her husband's ambitions for inheriting a fortune dashed, he took his bride to the West Indies, hoping to find employment there.

On New Providence she met Jack Rackham, who courted her away from her spouse. (Anne seems not to have been a model of fidelity.) She ran away to sea with him, disguised in male clothing. After some months she proved with child and, when her condition became obvious, Rackham took her to friends in Cuba who saw her through her accouchement. As soon as the child was born, she went back to sea with her lover. There is no record as to the disposition of her baby.

One time during his career, Rackham claimed the Act of Mercy; but with the slate of his past wiped clean, he soon returned to his old trade. It was shortly after this time that Anne Bonny and Mary Read first met. Despite their sex, they made a fierce pair of pirates, and in time of action, none "amongst them were more resolute, or ready to Board or undertake any Thing that was hazardous as she and Anne Bonny." One witness at their trial stated that the two cursed and swore with the best of males, and never cringed at murder. Their sex became known to the rest of the crew during this period, and the girls fancied female fashions until there was a possibility of action. Then they "dressed in men's jackets, and long trousers, and handkerchiefs tied about their heads," a costume more suitable for fighting.

An example of the raw courage of Mary Read came about after love had once again entered her life. She became enamoured of a young pirate who had been forced to serve in Rackham's crew. After they had become good friends, "she suffered the Discovery to be made, by carelessly shewing her Breasts, which were very White." And so began a shipboard romance, an event not customary on a pirate ship. Then, one day, Mary demonstrated her great affection in one of the "most generous Actions that ever Love inspired." There had been a quarrel involving her lover and a shipmate. According to pirate custom they were to be taken ashore to fight until blood was shed or one of the duellists died. Fearful of the results, Mary picked a quarrel with her lover's antagonist and challenged him two hours before he was to meet her boy. She duelled him "at Sword and Pistol" and left him dying.

When Rackham was captured, and after the fighting became hot, most of the crew fled down into the hold with the exception of Anne, Mary, and one other. Mary Read, shouting down the hatch, demanded that they come back and fight like men. When they remained cowering in the hold, she fired her pistols down into the crowd, killing one and wounding several others. And as fierce as was Mary Read, there is ample evidence to suggest that Anne Bonny was even more so.

After Rackham's crew were brought to trial, Mary's "Husband" (for she and her lover had privately plighted their troth) was able to prove he had been forced and was acquitted. Mary Read held no real fear of the noose for herself, and had once expressed the opinion to Calico Jack, "that as to hanging, she thought it no great Hardship, for, were it not for that, every cowardly Fellow would turn Pyrate, and so infest the Seas, that

"She duelled him 'at Sword and Pistol' and left him dying."

Men of Courage must starve . . . and no Merchant would venture out; so that the Trade, in a little Time, would not be worth following." But it was her "great Belly" that saved her from the gallows, but not from death. Although she was given a reprieve once she was found pregnant, soon afterwards she was seized with a violent fever and died in prison.

Anne Bonny, likewise found to be in the family way, was given a reprieve. Many of the island planters had been in Carolina and knew her father, and they gave her some help, although she was such a hardened baggage that she demonstrated scant appreciation. On the day that Rackham was to hang, he obtained permission to visit her. She gave little satisfaction to her former lover in the words, "that she was sorry to see him there, but if he had fought like a Man, he need not have been hang'd like a Dog."

Anne Bonny and her condemned lover, Calico Jack Rackham.

Anne remained in prison until she was delivered of her child. Afterwards she was reprieved from time to time until she disappeared. She was never hanged.

As more pirates were captured and hanged, the greater cruelty was practiced by those who were still alive. Perhaps the peak of pirate barbarity came around 1720 and was best exemplified in the persons of Captains George Lowther and Edward Low, both of whom sailed and plundered off the capes of Virginia. George Lowther had been a second mate on a slave ship belonging to the Royal African Company which he seized while off Gambia on the coast of Africa. He had taken many fine prizes in the Caribbean. Somewhere along the way he picked up his lieutenant, Edward Low. It was off Virginia that the two had parted company, with Low going off in the *Rebecca* of Boston, captured while en route to Virginia.

Lowther, in his *Happy Delivery,* captured several prizes off New York, and he first became known as one who delighted in torturing his prisoners. He and his men held a great fondness for the practice of placing lighted slow burning matches between the fingers of his victims, allowing them to burn the flesh to the bone if the prisoner did not reveal where his gold was hidden.

They ran into trouble off South Carolina when a prospective prize presented such a strong resistance that the pirates were forced aground. Lowther managed to get his ship off, but it was in such a shattered condition that he and his crew were forced to spend the winter of 1722–1723 in an isolated inlet of North Carolina, living on shore in tents while his ship was repaired.

The following summer he worked the sea lanes off Newfoundland. Once the weather turned cool he steered for the West Indies. While careened on the little island of Blanquilla, northeast of Tortuga, he was surprised and overwhelmed by the *Eagle,* a sloop out of Barbados, belonging to the South Sea Company. During the brisk fight a number of his crew were killed, with all but five of the survivors taken prisoner. Lowther, three seamen, and a small boy they used as a drummer escaped ashore. Lowther's end apparently came at his own hands, for he was later found dead on the beach, a burst pistol at his side.

It was Edward Low, however, who made piracy synonymous with cruelty, and he himself was condemned by many of his fraternity for giving their trade such a bad name. Low had been born in Westminster, England, and even as a lad had plundered the small boys of the neighborhood for their farthings. For several years he shipped out as an ordinary seaman before settling down to work in a Boston shipyard. Here he proved to be so cantankerous that he was discharged, and soon afterwards he found himself working with the log cutters in the Bay of Honduras. This employment was terminated when he angrily fired a musket at his captain and killed a bystander. Along with twelve companions in a small boat he fled out into the open sea where he "took a small Vessel . . . [to] make a black Flag, and declare War against all the World."

In the Grand Caymans he met George Lowther and was made that captain's lieutenant. He sailed with Lowther until May 28, 1722, when Low and forty-four others went off in the prize they had captured off Virginia. He was a daring captain, even slipping into protected harbors and cutting out choice prizes. In their operations Low and his crew ranged from New England to the West Indies, and as far eastward as the Azores, Madeiras, Cape Verde, and Canary islands. During his career, Low and his company took a minimum of ninety-three prizes, at least four of them off the Virginia coast. Some of the better-built and faster vessels were armed and added to his fleet if there were available men to man them. Low, it seems, refused to allow as many Negroes in his crew as did other captains. Free Negroes or mulattoes who voluntarily signed the articles were often sold into slavery.

In the beginning, Low's flag was unusual in that it was of blue cloth. Once he had gathered several ships under his command, however, he designed a distinctive black ensign with a red skeleton, as a symbol more befitting an admiral.

Low's appearance was as evil as his character. An accident added a diabolical leer to his features: One member of his crew, slashing at a prisoner with his cutlass, missed his mark and laid open Low's jaw. The ship's surgeon, already much gone in drink, sewed up the wound. When the captain found fault with his handiwork, the reeling surgeon struck Low in the face with such force that nearly all of the stitches were torn loose, and "then bid him sew up his Chops himself and be damned." And, it was noted, "Low made a very pitiful Figure for some time after."

The captain held a particular antipathy for prisoners from New England and Portugal, reserving his finest tortures for natives of those places. Although New England captains were not always murdered, Low's customary practice was to whip the naked man about the deck, slit his nose and nick him with his cutlass in various parts of the body. Then, if the prisoner appeared too badly hurt, he would be shot through the head to put him out of his misery. His crew seemed to delight as much as their chief in torture and mutilation. For instance, when a French prize was burned, they took off all of the crew except the cook, whom they bound to the mainmast and "who, they said, being a greasy Fellow would fry well in the Fire."

On one occasion they captured a Spanish pirate whose crew surrendered without resistance. Discovering six English sea captains held prisoner in the hold, Low's crew took a vote and then fell on the Spaniards with swords, cutlasses, pole-axes, and pistols. Many leaped overboard and swam for the shore, but a small boat was lowered and rowed among them, Low's men knocking the swimmers in the head as they struggled in the water. Twelve of them managed to make it to the shore and escape through the underbrush. One, too weak to continue his flight, crawled back to the shore and begged for mercy. One pirate grabbed him with, "G–d d—n him he would give him good Quarter presently," and thrust-

Massacre of the Spanish pirates by Edward Low and his bloodthirsty crew.

ing his fusil into the wounded man's mouth, fired it down his throat. In all, around forty-five of the Spanish pirates were massacred.

Atrocity seems to be too mild a word to apply to the treatment Low and his crew inflicted on their prisoners. One captain was decapitated, others were disembowelled. Two Portuguese friars were triced up to a yardarm and left hanging. Some of the punishments were downright ingenious in a grisly sort of way. After cutting off the ears of the captain of a New England whaler, Low sprinkled them with salt and pepper and then forced his victim to eat them. When one Portuguese captain was approached by the pirate captain, he hung a sack containing 11,000 gold moidores out of the window of his cabin. Just before his ship was taken, he cut the rope and allowed his treasure to drop into the sea. Low fell into a rage when he discovered how he had been deprived of the coin. Lashing the captain to the mast, he ordered the man's lips cut off and broiled before his eyes. Some accounts say that his mate was forced to eat them. Even then Low's anger raged unabated, and the entire Portuguese crew of thirty-two persons were massacred. Notwithstanding he lived in an age when brutality was customary, not many people thought Edward Low to be a very nice person.

As terrible and barbaric as Low might have been, he was still something of a coward. On June 10, 1723, Captain Peter Solgard of H.M.S. *Greyhound,* a guard ship out of New York, was on a routine cruise when she came upon Low in the *Fancy* and his consort ship, the *Ranger,* the latter under the command of Captain Charles Harris. The pirates, apparently not realizing the formidableness of the *Greyhound,* took her to be but another victim and gave chase. Solgard drew off, using the time to prepare for action. After two hours, the man-of-war came about and loosed a broadside. The *Ranger's* main yard was shot away. Low, rather than sailing in to aid his crippled companions, bore away before the wind, forcing Harris to beg for quarter. The crew of the *Ranger* were taken into Rhode Island, where Harris and twenty-seven members of his crew were hanged, including one Daniel Hyde of the eastern shore of Virginia.

No one knows for sure just what happened to Edward Low. He simply disappeared in the trackless wastes of the ocean. Some say that he went to Brazil; others declare that his ship, the *Merry Christmas,* sank with all hands. There is one story that Low, in a fit of anger, killed his quartermaster, and this so upset his crew that they deposed him and set him adrift in a small open boat along with three companions; he was picked up by a French warship, taken to Martinique and hanged. Although there is no clear evidence as to the eventual fate of Edward Low, no one mourned his passing—except, maybe, the Devil.

Few realized it at the time, but the passing of Roberts, Rackham, Vane, Lowther, Low, and their kind, marked an end to the Golden Age of Piracy.

VIII

THE WANING OF AN ERA

"neither the Land nor Waters can bear you longer"

From 1724 on, the majority of pirates operating off the North American coast were either foreigners or rank amateurs. The foreigners were Spanish, the Guardia de la Costa, acting beyond their territorial waters under commissions issued by the governors of Spanish colonial possessions. Since the peace of Utrecht in 1713 these people had plundered English shipping of goods valued at £300,000. They seemed to seek out slave ships as prizes.

In early June, 1724, three ships were taken off the Virginia capes by one crew of the Guardia de la Costa. They were a bold group. They cruised just below the horizon, out of the line of sight of the local guard ship, H.M.S. *Enterprize*. Once their intended victims became careless in their security, these pirates would swoop down on them. Their ship, the *St. Francis de la Vega,* was under the command of one who claimed to be a Spanish knight and called himself Don Benito. Its crew of nearly ninety men was made up of natives of Spain, England, France, and Ireland. Don Benito had an unusual agreement with the governor of Cuba, who had issued his commission and who owned the ship, which he hired out to Don Benito for a specified sum of money.

On June 25, 1724, Captain John James of the *John and Mary* spoke with the commander of the *Enterprize* and, assured that there were no pirates in the area, steered for the capes of Virginia. His cargo was 175 Negro slaves, but recently purchased on the African coast. Near sunrise a ship flying British colors was sighted. Jones, preparing to offer the customary courtesies of the sea, was arrested in his efforts as the stranger drew near with a loud hail of "God damn you, Strike, you English doggs, Strike!" From Jones's ship they took seventy-six prime slaves, gold dust, and personal clothing. The three female passengers aboard were not molested.

The next prize was a trim brigantine, the *Prudent Hannah,* out of Boston bound for Virginia with a cargo of merchandise. This ship, newly built and carrying a full set of sails, struck the fancy of the pirates who saw her as a "privateer" to add to their own strength. The following day they took the *Godolphin,* bound into the Rappahannock River. The captains of all three prizes were forced to remain on board the pirate ship until June 9 when the *Enterprize* was sighted on the horizon. All three were then placed aboard the *John and Mary* and allowed to go free. The *St. Francis de la Vega,* the *Prudent Hannah,* and the *Godolphin* sailed off on an eastward course.

The *Prudent Hannah* never became a pirate ship. Five pirates had been placed aboard her as a prize crew, along with three seamen of the *Prudent Hannah* who had been forced. Among the pressed men there was a short, dark complexioned, twenty-six year old foremast seaman, Mark Legaur. He was an Italian and spoke only broken English and harbored no ambitions towards becoming a pirate. During the night, while Legaur was standing his watch at the helm, he managed to slowly steer away from the running lights of the *St. Francis de la Vega* and lose the brigantine in the darkness. Stealing down into the cabin he discovered the commander of the prize crew dozing, two pistols beneath his head. Legaur, excusing himself on the grounds that he needed certain supplies, suddenly grabbed for the pistols. In the ensuing struggle, the pirate was shot and killed. The other members of the prize crew surrendered without resistance. Making their way to New York, the crew of the *Prudent Hannah* turned the pirates over to the authorities. Three were hanged, while one, a Frenchman, was acquitted on the premise that he had "Stood Neutral during the Action."

The most interesting amateur who operated off Virginia was one William Fly, whose career lasted less than six weeks. Fly, of Bristol, boxed with bare knuckles for prize money in his native England before turning to the sea. He had shipped out of Jamaica as a boatswain aboard the *Elizabeth,* bound for the Guinea coast to pick up a cargo of slaves.

Although some members of the crew were reluctant to turn pirate, Fly persuaded a majority to join him in mutiny and piracy. About one o'clock on the morning of May 27, 1726, they slipped out on deck and over-whelmed the helmsman. Those seamen who refused to join the conspiracy were thrown into irons. John Green, captain of the ship, was awakened and brought up on deck. There was much talk of throwing him overboard. Green, recognizing the cruelty pent up within Fly, knew full well that such threats were not made in jest and begged for his life. Falling upon his knees, the captain cried out that he had not prepared himself for death and that if his life was dispatched with such suddenness he would surely go to Hell.

Fly, impatient and impertinent, shouted for the Captain to repeat after him the words, "Lord, have mercy on my soul." No sooner had Green mumbled these words than he was picked up and thrown overboard. His hand, thrown out in desperation, grasped a trailing rope. One of the mutineers, Thomas Winthrop, spotted the captain and, taking up the cooper's broad axe, chopped off Green's hand, "and so he dropt into Eternity."

Thomas Jenkins, the mate, was next brought out on deck. Fly, in almost childish glee, told him that the captain had already been thrown overboard and as the two officers had messed together, they should now drink together. He was heaved overboard. Jenkins' last cries were for the ship's surgeon to throw him a line. But the surgeon was already in irons.

Fly renamed the *Elizabeth* the *Fame's Revenge* and set a course for the Carolina coast. He took the *John and Hannah* off Cape Hatteras, and when his prize crew had difficulty with the captured sloop, Fly blamed the captain and ordered him whipped. He also forced William Atkinson, an able navigator and mariner, to join his crew. Off the capes of Virginia, the *John and Mary* was taken and plundered.

Fly captured two more prizes before Atkinson was able to persuade several of the more unhappy members of the crew to join him in overpowering Fly and four of the ringleaders. Atkinson assumed command of the ship and carried the prisoners to Boston for trial. During the trial, Fly behaved himself "boldly and impenitently," and along with four others, was sentenced to die on the gallows. One of the condemned men,

George Condick, was reprieved for twelve months to obtain the King's mercy "in consideration that he was commonly intoxicated and an ignorant young man, and mostly employed as cook on board the snow Elizabeth."

Fly refused to attend the special sermon preached for the pirates, thereby failing to hear the Reverend Benjamin Coleman castigate his profession with "you drown your Souls in destruction and perdition; turning robbers and murderers till neither the Land nor Waters can bear you longer." Fly, whatever he considered his role in life to be, played it to the end. On Tuesday, July 12, 1726, with the traditional nosegay of flowers in his manacled hands, he leaped briskly into the cart that was to transport him to the gallows, "bowing with much unconcern to the Spectators as he pass'd along, and at the Gallows he behaved still obstinately and boldly till his face was covered for death."

The year 1727 was the last in which pirates were to play any significant role in Virginia and most of the mainland colonies. In that year seven sloops were taken off the Virginia coast by the Spanish Guardia de la Costa operating out of Havana. As late as 1731, Governor William Gooch was complaining of the decay into which the river forts had been allowed to fall, and demanding protection "against the insults of Pirates which we have reason to expect from the usual increase from that kind of Vermin in times of Peace." His fears, in general, were unfounded. The very fact that the forts had been allowed to crumble is an indication that there was no longer any great fear of an incursion of pirates.

Some piratical activity had occurred just before Gooch's arrival in Virginia, and he was there in time to see it terminated. John Vidal, "a man of Desperate fortune," gathered a small group around him and set out in a small open boat to plunder ships coming into Ocracoke Inlet. But the people of that community had grown weary of pirates and some of the "Country people" set upon this gang and captured Vidal, two members of his crew, and one other man who had been forced to join them.

The authorities of North Carolina held no authority to try pirates, although they did consider bringing Vidal and his companions before the General Court as ordinary felons. Eventually the four men, along with the proper witnesses, were dispatched to Virginia for trial before the court of vice-admiralty.

The forced man was acquitted, but John Vidal and his two men were condemned to die on the gallows. The two ordinary seamen were hanged, but it appears that Vidal, "an Irish man & a Protestant," was a person of some substance. He was well acquainted with Richard Fitzwilliam, as other pirates before him had been. Other influential men worked quietly in his behalf. Vidal likewise submitted an eloquent appeal and lament, detailing his fall from grace as a result of "the tenderness of youth in being overtaken by the temptations of the world together with the late loss I sustained by the master of my vessel, who run away with her from Potomack in Maryland, with her load of Tobacco put me quite out of ever seeing my Dear parents, which threw me in Dispair and melancholly . . . this finishing stroke of my misfortune almost bereaved me of my senses, which God forgive me for it, but I never intended to go a pirating." His plea was for time as this would be "a grate benefit to my poor soul which must answer before the great tribunal of heaven, for all my Sins Done in the Body—what a comfortable thing it is for a Dying man to have a little time to make his peace with God." Such florid rhetoric seems to have touched the hearts of some, or else it was seized upon as a proper reason for reprieve by Robert Carter, president of the Council and acting governor.

After the arrival of Governor Gooch, one of the first topics discussed in Council was the case of John Vidal. It was unanimously agreed that Vidal was a fit subject for the King's mercy, and the Council suggested that it would be a most fitting gesture if Vidal were pardoned out of respect for the accession of George II to the throne of England. They also suggested to Gooch that it would be "very becoming" to begin his colonial administration with an act of mercy. Vidal received his pardon. Even then, this accused pirate did not have the necessary funds to pay his prison and other fees and money had to be appropriated before he could be freed. Vidal seems to have remained in Virginia, for some years later a man by that name was living on the Pamunkey River in King William County.

If there has to be a specific date for the end of the era known as the Golden Age of Piracy, it would be 1728. Official correspondence up to that date is filled with details of, and concerns about piracy, but the word is seldom mentioned after 1728. From that year on there would be frequent alarms, and an occasional ship would be taken, but in general the seas became relatively clear of the depredations by the freebooters.

The beginning of the end might be said to have come in 1721 when the piracy act was broadened to include as accessories those who traded with pirates. This had eliminated many markets for the sale of plunder, and pirates were not so openly welcomed in port towns as they had been back around the turn of the century. So long as they had operated in the Caribbean and the Far East, there had been no great odium attached to dealings with pirates, but there had been a great change of heart when they began to plunder merchant vessels along the mainland coast of North America. Equally important as a factor in the demise of piracy had been the gradual exclusion of pirates from their West Indian bases. In later years there had been an attempt to establish another pirate haven in North Carolina, but this had been put down by the local people after the Board of Trade, noting that the colony had long "been a Receptacle for Pyrates, Thieves and Vagabonds of all sorts," recommended that North Carolina be made a district of Virginia.

Equally effective in the suppression of piracy was the revocation of proprietary charters by the Crown. In general, this brought better government and more carefully selected governors. In those colonies where the proprietors were allowed to retain their charters, they insisted on more stringent measures against pirates and piracy for fear their charters would become subject to revocation.

In the West Indies, the captains of the guard ships were chosen with greater care. No longer did they exploit their position by selling convoy duty or engaging in personal trading. In May, 1722, the governor of Jamaica thought it "a very fortunate accident" when one guard ship captured fifty-eight pirates, forty-one of whom were hanged. One of the most active naval commanders in the pursuit of pirates on the West Indian station was Captain Ellis Brand, who had been sent out in H.M.S. *Hector*. Captain Solgard of the guard ship stationed at New York was equally energetic in his operations against pirates off the mainland and boldly attacked all those who ventured within his cruising range. Indirect aid came from the efforts of Captain Chaloner Ogle, commander of the sixty-two gun ship of the line, *Swallow,* who was to be knighted for clearing the African coast of pirates, the most notable being Bartholomew Roberts. And not to be discounted were those merchant ships that were refitted and commissioned as privateers against pirates in the West Indies.

Only when England and her colonies put behind them the idea that they could afford crime better than they could afford an adequate police force did affairs take a turn for the better. Merchants in the home country were effective in their influence on the government to remove the causes of economic isolation in the colonial trade.

Put in its simplest terms, once a congenial atmosphere was eliminated, piracy collapsed of its own weight.

A Word About Sources

A WORD ABOUT SOURCES

No one seems quite positive about the true identity of the author who signed himself as Captain Charles Johnson and who published, in 1724, a volume entitled, *A General History of the Pyrates From Their first Rise and Settlement in the Island of Providence, to the present Time.* Some have identified Johnson as Daniel Defoe and he is sometimes so identified in library card catalogues. Whoever the author, his account has provided the framework for every book on piracy since the date of its publication. Johnson must have had some access to the official correspondence of the day, for much of the information, even conversation, is corroborated in both personal correspondence and official dispatches. The greatest disparity was in the account of Richard Worley who Johnson states was killed in Virginia waters rather than off the South Carolina coast, but this mistake was corrected in later editions. Sketches of the more noted pirates were included, verbatim, in Johnson's later publication (1734) of the *General History of the Lives and Adventures of the most famous Highwaymen, to which is added Voyages and Plunder of the most notorious Pyrates.* Because of the era in which Johnson did his work and its close correlation with the official records, his *History of the Pyrates* must be considered as a basic work.

Printed sources that proved valuable, especially with regard to the buccaneers, included, John Esquemeling, *The Buccaneers of America: A True Account of the Most Remarkable Assaults Committed of Late Years upon the Coasts of the West Indies by the Buccaneers of Jamaica and Tobago (Both English and French)*, (London, 1951. Reprint of the English version of 1684), and Louis de Golif, *The Memoirs of a Buc-*

caneer: Being a Wondrous and Unrepentant Account of the Prodigious Adventures and Amours of King Louis XIV's Loyal Servant Adhémar Timothée Le Golif ·known for his singular wound as Borgnefesse Captain of the Buccaneers, Told by Himself, edited by G. Alaux and A. t'Serstevens and translated by Malcolm Barnes (London, 1954).

I was fortunate enough to find a number of contemporary printed accounts of the trials of various pirates including those of William Kidd, Stede Bonnet, Samuel Bellamy, Charles Harris, William Fly, and John Quelch, the majority of which were in the William L. Clements Library. Printed hanging-day sermons contain more than righteous homilies and incorporate a number of details of piratical activities. Two such discourses that were particularly helpful are in the Clements Library: Benjamin Coleman, *A Sermon Preached to Some Miserable Pirates, July 10, 1726, On the Lord's Day before their Execution* (Boston, 1726) and Cotton Mather, *Instructions to the Living from the Condition of the Dead. A Brief Relation of Remarkables in the Shipwreck of above One Hundred Pirates, Who were Cast away in the Ship Whido, on the Coast of New England, April 26, 1717* (Boston, 1717). A similar document is *An Account of the Behaviour and last Dying Speeches of the Six Pirates, that were Executed on Charles River, Boston side, on Fryday, June 30, 1704* (Boston, 1704).

Much material, although in abbreviated form, may be found in the various volumes of the *Calendar of State Papers, Colonial Series, America and West Indies* (London, 1862–   ). Official action and concern with pirates is included in H. R. McIlwaine and Wilmer L. Hall, editors, *Executive Journals of the Council of Colonial Virginia* (Richmond, 1925–45), and H. R. McIlwaine, editor, *Journals of the House of Burgesses of Virginia* (Richmond, 1906–15). Scattered references are in William L. Saunders, editor, *The Colonial Records of North Carolina* (Raleigh, 1886–90), William P. Palmer and others, editors, *Calendar of Virginia State Papers and Other Manuscripts, 1652–1781* (Richmond, 1875), *The William and Mary Quarterly, The Virginia Magazine of History and Biography, The Pennsylvania Magazine of History and Biography,* the *South Carolina Historical Collections,* and *Tyler's Historical and Genealogical Magazine.*

For the Blackbeard story, the one indispensable work is R. A. Brock, editor, *The Official Letters of Alexander Spotswood, Lieutenant-Governor of the Colony of Virginia, 1710–1722* (Richmond, 1932–35).

From Chapter III on, considerable manuscript materials in the microfilm of the Virginia Colonial Records Project were available at Colonial Williamsburg. The majority of manuscripts used were from the Colonial Office, the Admiralty, and the Treasury, deposited in the Public Record Office. Much of the information relative to the battle between the *Shoreham* and the *La Paix* was included in the many depositions from the Rawlinson manuscripts of the Bodleian Library in Oxford. Some material was found in the Blathwayt papers of Colonial Williamsburg, Inc., the Wedderburn papers of the William L. Clements Library, and the Thomas Pollock Letterbook in the North Carolina Department of Archives and History.

Three secondary works on pirates were of great value; Philip Gosse, *The History of Piracy* (3rd edition, New York, 1946), Patrick Pringle, *Jolly Roger: The Story of the Great Age of Piracy* (New York, 1953), and James Burney, *History of the Buccaneers of America* (reprint of the 1816 edition, London, 1951). Other studies furnished the information for specific incidents or the basis for broader generalizations. These include H. A. Ormerod, *Piracy in the Ancient World* (Chicago, 1957), Shirley Carter Hughson, *The Carolina Pirates and Colonial Commerce* (Baltimore, 1894), Don C. Seitz, *Under the Black Flag* (New York, 1925), Cyrus H. Karraker, *Piracy was a Business* (Rindge, N.H., 1953), Harold T. Williams, *Captain Kidd and his Skeleton Island: The Discovery of a Strange Secret Hidden for 266 Years* (London, 1937), and William Hallam Bonner, *Pirate Laureate: The Life & Legends of Captain Kidd* (New Brunswick, 1957).

Other studies not directly concerned with piracy, but which proved useful included Alexander Brown, *The Genesis of the United States* (Boston, 1890), Philip Alexander Bruce, *Institutional History of Colonial Virginia in the Seventeenth Century* (New York, 1910), Herbert L. Osgood, *The American Colonies in the Eighteenth Century* (New York, 1930) and M. Eugene Sirmans, *Colonial South Carolina: A Political History, 1663–1763* (Chapel Hill, 1966).

Studies found useful for peripheral details included W. G. Perrin, *British Flags* (Cambridge, 1922) and R. G. Marsden, editor, *Documents Relating to Law and Custom of the Sea* (London, 1915).

Although this volume is not footnoted, a documented manuscript is on deposit in the Archives, Colonial Williamsburg, Inc., Williamsburg, Virginia.

Index

INDEX